THE AMERICAN DREAM 2.0

THE AMERICAN DREAM 2.0

SEWING TOGETHER OLD SCHOOL TECHNIQUES WITH NEW SCHOOL TECHNOLOGY

CRAIG SEWING

CRAIG SEWING MEDIA

THE AMERICAN DREAM 2.0

Sewing Together Old School Techniques with New School Technology

ISBN 978-1-5445-0714-9 *Hardcover*

978-1-5445-0713-2 *Paperback*

978-1-5445-0712-5 *Ebook*

This book is dedicated to my Mom and Dad,

My heroes who gave me the foundation to pursue my dreams.

CONTENTS

PART 4: THE AMERICAN DREAM 2.0: *YOUR STORY*

INTRODUCTION

Is the American dream dead?

This is the question I was asked on 9-11-2018 by a radio host.

My response: "Are you dead?"

I got a blank stare. Maybe you're not supposed to answer a question, with another question. But the truth is, the moment we stop dreaming is the moment we might as well be.

The media often asks this question about The American Dream. Why? Well, because they don't have much substance in their content, and just try and spark debate. Negative and nauseating.

But who cares about the media. Journalism is dead, and it lost its way a LONG time ago. I am more concerned about you living out your dreams!

It all starts with mindset, and until you believe in yourself and your own dreams, you can't expect others to.

With that statement, I'm starting this book with the confident statement, we are living in the greatest era for achievement, ever.

The American dream.

No, it's not dead.

It's right there for you if you simply have the ambition to achieve your version of it—whatever that looks like.

Think it, feel it, believe it, and live it like you own it already. Your mindset, and your peace of mind, comes from within, not from anything you ever chase externally. The American dream has a subjective meaning; you get to choose what it looks like for you.

YOU decide!

You've already won the lottery of life being born here. This continues to be the greatest land for freedom and opportunity that exists. Now, I don't mean that in a "hell yeah...'Merica man!!" kinda way. But seriously, there is a reason that people want *into* this country, not out of it.

No matter how big your aspirations, it's equally important to make sure you enjoy the journey, because if you have big goals, it won't be easy. There is no magic pill. You gotta enjoy all the ups *and* downs. That's the whole "you only live one life" thing. If you don't enjoy the process and experience, you're chasing a pipe dream into an endless tunnel with no real destination.

I truly want you to first start with the state of mind that you aren't *chasing* your American dream...You are living it and simply growing its meaning and significance through your positive impact on the world. Your success will be measured by the radius of that impact.

Some might find that whole "we live in the greatest country" comment to be biased or even arrogant.

It's really not meant to be.

Earlier I suggested that there is a reason people want *into* this country, not out of it. I should've said, *MILLIONS* of people want into it, not out of it. Some even risk their lives trying, while we have unappreciative people here who binge-watch Netflix complaining how hard it is.

A few other key thoughts:

- You get paid more on welfare in the United States than doctors in other parts of the world.
- Whether you're disabled, retired, a veteran, or even just unemployed, there is financial support for you.
- As you read this, there is a voluntary military, composed of real people, willing to *die* to protect your freedom. Think about that for a moment—voluntarily!

There is no time for excuses in a place like this.

You're already living a dream life that millions upon millions would wish for.

And just being born in itself is a one-in-a-gazillion chance.

So the question is, what do you want to make of it?

At this point in time, any excuse is bullshit.

And if believing you live in the greatest country on the planet is a biased statement, oh well.

I also believe I have the greatest mom on the planet. There are certain things in life you are allowed to be biased about. I hope you feel the same way.

And the truth is, if you were born in Mexico, Brazil, France, the deserts of the Middle East...it doesn't matter. The moment you stop dreaming is the moment you're dead.

This negative media nonsense suggesting "the American dream is dead" is just a talking head desperate for something to talk about. Most of them can't even communicate without a teleprompter.

To think dreaming is dead, whether it be as individuals, or collectively as a nation, is the ultimate self-fulfilling prophecy. Have we really become so cynical or obsessed with the negative messaging our media puts out there that we question our ability to dream?

Some of the most life-changing words in our history were "I have a dream," by Dr. Martin Luther King Jr. And with all these incredible freedoms, if you still don't believe this is the greatest nation on earth, you also have the freedom to leave. Simple.

Since we're just getting to know each other...If you haven't figured it out already, I tend to get fired up. I am delusionally passionate and known to wear my heart on my sleeve.

Just like you, I am always in pursuit of advancing my American dream.

My goal with this book is to inspire you with real stories and strategies.

I got nothing but love for you, and I don't even know you. You're reading my book! Time is your most valuable asset, and the fact that you are giving me some of yours is the ultimate compliment. Thank you.

Much of what you will read in this book are real stories I have experienced—mostly relating to my experiences as an entrepreneur, playing in the media space. Simply put, it's me; it's what I know.

My hope is to find a connection with you, where even if you find yourself in a different space, you can translate the content to make it relatable to your world. When I say entrepreneur, it could easily be translated to anyone chasing their dreams, trailblazing, and making their own rules. When I say media, we should all understand that this is the ultimate media landscape. *Everything* is tied to media, whether you consume it or leverage it.

While I might be the creator of a TV show called *The American Dream* and CEO of a media company, *you* absolutely must understand the media space, because it's not just the traditional TV shows. We live in a fascinating world of digital and social media—easily the greatest time in the history of humankind to have the ability to make connections, build relationships, and achieve. And you...you are the CEO of YOU in this journey.

American Dream 2.0 is a compilation of real stories and life lessons, tailored to this insane technologically advanced world we find ourselves in. And no, it is not some phony "ghostwritten" book written by someone else claiming as my own. My own fingers are crushing a keyboard, with sleepless nights till I get the right message to you, one that I've spent decades accumulating knowledge for.

Because even though we have an amazing future in this opportunistic world of technological advancement for which to accomplish our American dream, there is still something very meaningful about our past.

The things that got us here, that are often ignored.

The new school puts a smartphone in your hand and gives you connectivity to the world, people, and knowledge.

But without old-school heart, hustle, relationships, and love, you're missing all the key ingredients to thrive in today's world. With this book, we will *sew* it all together (yes, pun intended, with my last name being Sewing).

You will become the inspiration and executioner of your

American dream. It's your dream. It's your responsibility. It's yours to get.

But updated for today's environment.

This ain't your grandparents' world. In fact, life is moving so fast that it's not even your parents' world. Things look dramatically different than they did just a matter of a few years ago.

I call it *American Dream 2.0.*

Sewing together old-school techniques with new-school technology.

You ready?

Then let's stop ranting, and get started.

I'm fired up!

I'm going to go meditate (a key message in this book), find my Zen, and come back and pour my heart and soul into this book for you.

Ready?

Let's GO!

PART 1

———

THE AMERICAN DREAM 1.0 VERSUS THE AMERICAN DREAM 2.0

CHAPTER 1

* * *

THEY DON'T SERVE SALAD AT THE SALAD BOWL

The Salad Bowl was a beloved Saint Louis business. More specifically, it was a cafeteria. Its success was not one of those things you can measure. Just like its food, the restaurant itself had a great recipe—one built on the ingredients of relationships and having a great story.

The Salad Bowl first opened in 1948, on Lindell Boulevard in the Central West End neighborhood of Saint Louis. At the time, it was a predominantly African American neighborhood, and so were its customers and employees. To hear that today might not sound like a big deal, except for one thing: this was the 1940s, and the Salad Bowl was owned by a white man...a gentleman by the name of Elmer.

In the '40s, '50s, and '60s—when the American dream meant something quite a bit different—serving meals to white people and black people side by side wasn't exactly common. Desegregation hadn't exactly happened.

But that's what Elmer did. He was a man of principle.

Even in the prejudiced time he lived in—long before the civil rights era and even decades before Martin Luther King Jr.'s "I Have a Dream" speech—Elmer knew that people of all colors were equal in every way. In fact, Elmer was once quoted as saying, "We will serve anyone who wants a hot meal, regardless of color."

The key ingredient: relationships.

Elmer was my grandfather.

A man I never met.

This is the story of the Salad Bowl, but there are many, many others just like it across America.

After establishing the Salad Bowl's legacy, he passed it down to my father, David Sewing, and his two brothers, Norman and Norbert Sewing, in the late '60s, supported by their wives, Julie, Susan, and Doris, respectively. And despite modern-day divorces averaging 60-plus percent, they all remained married. The women behind these men are as important as the story itself. Julie Sewing, aka Mom, is the unsung hero who was there every step of the way, through all the ups and downs.

At the Salad Bowl, they continued to serve people with the same respect Elmer had given their first patrons, continuously building their American dream on the foundation of kindness and relationships.

These men employed handicapped people, those who were deaf, young and old, black and white, and anyone ambitious enough to join the family and succeed. More importantly, this was also the environment they created with their customers.

A key thesis of this entire book is the importance of relationships, even in a digital world.

Building authentic relationships is the most important part of living the American dream.

I went to the Salad Bowl many times growing up, but one visit is etched into my memory—it's when I came face-to-face with the American dream for the first time.

It was a humid summer evening in the '80s, and I was just a young Cardinals fan eager to catch a game with my dad. In Saint Louis, Cardinal baseball is a religion of its own.

My mom dropped me off at the Salad Bowl to meet my dad. He came out smelling like a cafeteria and wearing his white shirt and tie, just like he did every day. This was pretty much his uniform.

He'd spent the entire day the same way his father had before him—working hard, serving his customers, and building authentic relationships. Every day, he sat with his customers and shared a meal with them, sharing stories and building friendships.

Before we left for the game, we went into the cafeteria to grab a bite to eat. He didn't grab my meal for me, nor did he send me to his back office to eat it. Instead, he put me in the long cafeteria line with his customers and made me wait through it, grabbing my meal, piece by piece, until we reached the cash register.

Like I said, everyone was equal in the Salad Bowl—no preferential treatment, not even for the owner's son.

Odie, one of the men who worked in the kitchen, would holler at me from behind the cafeteria line, poking his head through a window in the kitchen: "Young man, you gonna take over this for your father?" In fact, I heard similar questions from nearly every cook down the line. Their kindness to me was an expression of admiration for my dad.

When I arrived at the cash register, there was Millie waiting to ring us up, just like she did for so many others for fifty years. (You read that correctly: this woman worked loyally at this restaurant for *fifty years*. Wrap your head around that for a second!)

My dad and I sat in the main dining room, chatting with customers while we ate our meal.

He and his brothers did this almost every single day. What a lesson I was being taught and didn't even realize it.

Finally, it was game time!

My dad carried his old, brown, beat-up AM radio so we could listen to Jack Buck calling the game while we sat in Busch Stadium. Seems funny when you look back at it, but Jack was so good we just had to listen to his radio broadcast. These days, it's all about podcasts, but there was nothing like listening to Jack Buck call a game.

I don't remember if Ozzie Smith made a diving play at short, or if Bruce Sutter came in to pitch the ninth. I don't even remember if the Cardinals won or lost.

What I will always remember was the time with my dad and the people I met at the Salad Bowl. That's how I learned what really matters in the American dream: relationships.

WHAT HAPPENED TO THE AMERICAN DREAM 1.0?

My dad never taught me not to swear.

He just didn't swear.

He didn't teach me how to treat women.

He just treated my sisters, mom, and all women with respect.

He didn't teach me how to be an amazing dad.

He was just an amazing dad himself.

He wasn't a man of many words.

He was a man of simple actions.

In today's age, so many people have to say how great they are, rather than just simply being great.

Whether he knew, I can look back on that day at the Salad Bowl and going to the Cardinals game, and see something truly amazing: this was his American dream.

While the food was good at the Salad Bowl, they were known for their relationships and how they made people *feel*. People will remember you by how you made them feel.

The Salad Bowl was where people went after church. They had birthdays there, anniversaries, banquets— everything. It was accessible to people from all walks of life, regardless of the color of their skin, their age, their religion, or if they happened to be disabled, deaf, or homeless. It didn't matter. The Salad Bowl was a home away from home for them. The funny thing is, they didn't even really serve salad! But just like a real salad bowl has a mixture of ingredients, so did this cafeteria.

My dad and his brothers embodied the American Dream 1.0, and they had amazing values: hard work, honesty, and giving more than they received.

But just like so much of the American Dream 1.0, as a country we have completely disposed of places like the Salad Bowl.

The Salad Bowl doesn't exist anymore. Sold and later crushed by a wrecking ball, it's been replaced by an apartment building.

And as for other mom-and-pop shops, retailers like the Walmarts, Applebee's, and Ace Hardwares of the world came in and made everything cheaper and quicker, which drove family businesses out.

Change is necessary—and as a country we've advanced in a lot of ways since the days of the Salad Bowl—but perhaps some of those mom-and-pop shops still leave a ripple effect in their legacy.

They built their successes from *relationships* and having a great story that people talked about.

We've traded handshakes for emails and word of mouth for online reviews.

Where does that leave us? Maybe feeling a bit empty, but perhaps this creates *opportunity*.

A new kind of American dream: American Dream 2.0, where you combine old-school techniques with new-school technology.

THE AMERICAN DREAM 2.0

Our parents' generation did a lot of things right—they worked hard, they had manners, and they built relationships. But they also made mistakes.

The American Dream 1.0 promised a steady career. It

meant marrying your high school sweetheart. It meant going to college and buying a home with that white picket fence.

That dream worked back then.

It's not working anymore.

That was then; this is now.

The game has changed.

This is the best time in the history of humankind to be alive, and the best opportunities continue to exist in the greatest country: the United States of America.

The new American dream allows you to define your own reality, not have it defined for you.

It's your choice.

What's your story gonna be?

MY INTENTIONS WITH THIS BOOK

Entrepreneur is literally the most overused word of the twenty-first century. Okay, I take that back—the most overused word literally is *literally*. (Thanks, Kardashians.

I think I even used it earlier. Excuse me while I vomit in my mouth a little.)

Everybody wants to be an entrepreneur. Everyone hears about the online world and the freedom to live your passion. People are working for themselves more than ever in America. That's great. You could even call me a serial entrepreneur. I love the spirit of entrepreneurship.

But along with the influx of entrepreneurs has come an explosion of *want*repreneurs.

The posers. Those who think we live in a shortcut kinda world.

While the modern-day environment creates an abundance of opportunity, it does not excuse hard work.

I mean, seriously, how many wannabe twenty-something-year-old life coaches are there now? You know, who teaches you about life? Um, *life*.

The increase in wantrepreneurs has led to an entire landscape of the internet flooded with get-rich-quick schemes: "Sign up and pay for my webinar, and I'll show you how to make a million dollars doing webinars."

Most of them are bullshit.

This book is not the equivalent of a get-rich-quick scheme. I'll leave that to the modern-day snake oil salesman living behind their computer screen. Truth is that even today, with all the opportunities the internet allows us, there are no shortcuts.

The ingredients of the American Dream 1.0 are the same ingredients that will fan your fire for success today: hard work, building relationships, having passion and a purpose.

In this book, I'll give you real stories and actionable advice to build your business and your relationships. While the internet allows for incredible digital connection, the truth is, real business and real relationships are cemented in person—with a handshake.

As you read, you'll find inspiration from stories of real people just like you who are striving for the American Dream 2.0.

None of the people in this book took a shortcut, and none of them let the outside world define their dream.

When it's your dream, it's *your* dream.

It's up to *you* to get it.

CHAPTER 2

★ ★ ★

THE ROCKING CHAIR OF COMPLACENCY

The American Dream 1.0 has its place in history.

But today, it's like a rocking chair. It's sturdy, reliable, and safe, but when you stand up forty years from now, you'll realize that you spent decades rocking back and forth without actually moving anywhere.

Lou Holtz, the famous Notre Dame football coach, once said, "Like a blade of grass, in life you're either growing or dying."

You were put on this planet to grow. You were born to move beyond what your parents did, no matter how noble it was. There's nothing inherently wrong with our parents' American dream, but today's world is different.

If you want to excel—if you want to live the American Dream 2.0—you have to do something different. The first step is acknowledging that the landscape always changes, regardless of your industry. Change is always a constant, but these days it happens at an unprecedented speed.

Some people despise change. You want to be successful? Embrace change. It's the one constant thing that gives you an edge. Just keep paying attention and moving forward with it.

There is no "right path of life," and even if there were, I am *certainly* not one to judge what's right for you.

My issue is with those who complain about their life but aren't willing to acquire the knowledge or skills that could alter their course or take them to the next level. Complacency, or rocking in the chair, is fine—unless it's complacency with *complaints*.

And to be clear, there's nothing inherently wrong with some of the American Dream 1.0 way of doing things: going to college, marrying young, sticking with one job, and buying your little piece of land. For some people, that *is* the American dream. If you're happy with that, great. God bless ya!

But if you want a different life, you have to work to change it, which starts with getting out of that proverbial rocking chair.

I am *not* sitting here pontificating about how great my advice is while I type out this book. The truth is, I'm still *very much* in the hustle, every day. This book comes from my heart, a place of passion, and an excitement for sharing some things that can in some way, shape, or form enhance your life. The moment I stop chasing my dream is the moment I shouldn't be writing a book encouraging you to do the same.

The truth is, I'm working just like you, striving for the American Dream 2.0.

ACTION ITEMS

Get the goals out of your head and onto a piece of paper. Write your goals in a journal, a Post-it Note on the bathroom mirror, a vision board. I don't care *how* you do it; just *stop* thinking about it, and *start* doing it.

• What are your goals?

• What does your American Dream 2.0 look like?

• What's holding you back from your American Dream 2.0?

• What steps do you need to take to make progress *today*? One step at a time.

Take it from a thought to a visual, and write it out.

Do it every day. The hardest part is getting started. Step 1: Get clarity, get out of the gate, build momentum.

* * *

THERE IS NO GOLDEN TICKET

You remember that classic movie *Willy Wonka & the Chocolate Factory?*

In the beginning of the movie, Charlie peels back the foil of a chocolate bar, hoping for the slightest hint of a golden glitter underneath.

Will we find a golden ticket and have our dreams come true, or will this be just another ordinary chocolate bar? Charlie struck gold. Lucky guy.

Unfortunately, there are no golden tickets to the American Dream 2.0, unless you win the lottery, in which case, good luck chasing Powerballs. There wasn't one in the American Dream 1.0 days either.

I never graduated college.

It would be easy to say I'm a college dropout; at least that would mean I had more choice in the matter. But it's more accurate to say that my university didn't want me as a student anymore. Kicked out—a little different than dropped out. Less glorious.

I was twenty-one years old, paying $200 a month rent, and living with three roommates who still went to school. I went from college dropout to full-time career *instantly* kinda by accident, but that's where I found myself at an early age. The hustle started while I was still living in the middle of one big party.

I remember sleeping in my room while the party raged on into the night upstairs, only to wake up for work at 6:00 a.m. the next day, with drunk people passed out on the couch.

Don't get me wrong, I liked a good party, and you can absolutely learn a ton in college. I'm not one of those people saying, "Screw college." But your diploma won't be your golden ticket to success. And you're pretty much guaranteed to come out with debt.

It all starts with taking a hard look in the mirror and recognizing if you want a different path; it's on you to make it happen.

Truth is, I never would've been successful going through college and working my way up a corporate ladder. For me, it just wasn't in my DNA. And truth is, for most college kids, college is not the stepping-stone many pretend it to be.

That's the harsh truth, and universities are lying to their students about it while the students bankroll their salaries.

Robert Kiyosaki, author of *Rich Dad, Poor Dad*, states it bluntly: "You can climb the corporate ladder, or can just build your own."

The American Dream 2.0 isn't for people who wait for permission or expect a handout. It's for the trailblazers. The internet and that little computer in your hand you call a smartphone is the closest thing you have to a golden ticket. It's the gateway to opportunity.

Why? Knowledge has never been more accessible.

In the American Dream 1.0, you had to walk to the library and find your intelligence through endless reading. In the American Dream 2.0, it's a punch of a touch-screen button.

ACTION ITEMS

You can make a lot of money working for a corporate giant. You can show up every day uninspired, unmotivated, and dispirited. But you'll walk away with some money and perceived security. Plenty of people are happy with that life, but the market crash of 2008 proved that there is no such thing as security.

However, if the idea of working for a corporate giant makes you sick to your stomach, I've got good news: you're not alone. There are plenty of us out here who looked up at the corporations, like David facing Goliath, and calmly said, "No, thanks. I'll go my own way."

It's a high-risk, high-reward proposition. But if you're like me, you take that risk because you accept that you get only one life.

And when you lie on your deathbed one day, you'll want to look back and know you went for it all, despite the risk.

Write this down.

- What does your ideal life look like?

- What would you be doing every day?

- What line of work would you not even consider to be work but rather your passion?

- What keeps you from making this a reality?

- What steps do you need to take for *that* life?

Remember the old saying, "How do you eat an elephant?"

One bite at a time.

Think big. What does it look like? No reverse engineering it.

What does step 1 look like?

Let's take that first step *today*.

CHAPTER 4

HIDING BEHIND THE COMPUTER SCREEN

You see them littering the internet like overturned trash cans spilling garbage into the street.

"How to Build a Seven-Figure Online Business Working from Home"

"Make Six Figures in Your Sleep in Three Easy Steps"

"Sign Up for Our Webinar and Learn How to Earn Supplemental Income by Doing Webinars"

Each one leads to a sales funnel, coaxing you to pay hundreds of dollars for their "secrets" to online business success. They are the modern-day equivalent of snake oil salesmen, and they all promise you a fast path to fortune without ever leaving the comfort of your screen.

Almost every single one is bullshit.

THERE IS NO SHORTCUT TO HARD WORK.

And while modern-day technology leads to knowledge, connectivity, and opportunities we've never seen before, there are some things you just can't do behind a computer screen.

> The American Dream 1.0 got this part right, and all of us can take note: relationships, manners, and face-to-face connection will always win over the online game.
>
> PASSION + HARD WORK + BUILDING RELATIONSHIPS = OPPORTUNITY FOR SUCCESS

CHAPTER 5

* * *

SPRINTING ON FLAT GROUND

Let's be clear, hard work still counts in the American Dream 2.0, just like it did in the American Dream 1.0. There's just way more opportunity now than ever. Now, I realize you're probably thinking, "Okay, I get it. Hard work. Yeah, I get it." But honestly, so many people don't. Sending a bunch of emails confusing motion with action is not hard work. There is a big difference between busy-ness and business.

But now that we live in an environment with so much opportunity, the "sprinters" in the world can stop running up a mountain and find themselves on flat ground. Just the opportunity to connect alone holds significant value, in comparison to our not-so-distant past.

You can reach out to CEOs through LinkedIn, you can geotarget content to your ideal audience on Facebook and Instagram, and you can learn new skills by typing a few words into Google or YouTube.

Want to learn how to cook Thai food?

Play the guitar?

Speak Spanish?

You can do it from your smartphone, *right now*.

Never before has there been a time when you can learn something, practically instantly, with a few keyboard clicks. (Hell, YouTube can give you a better education than an accredited university.)

This is about grabbing your market share and building new success strategies to succeed in your business. ***You cannot gain market share without being a great marketer...and today's world is a marketer's dream!***

To do that, pay attention to what's happening in the world around you.

The game has changed.

And so should you.

Hard work is still admirable, but how you *execute* that hard work is the new differentiator. Before, you had to haul your ass up a mountain to create an opportunity and capitalize on it (aka the corporate ladder). The titans of industry looked down on you from their perches atop the mountain and gave corporate speeches: "Do you want to reach our pinnacle of success?" Building *their* dreams.

You might have shouted, "Yes!" into the sky. You might have squeaked it under your voice. Either way, you couldn't run your way up that mountain; you had to *trudge* your way up it.

Today, with the advances of the internet and social media, we're not climbing a mountain anymore. There are opportunities everywhere. Now the hard work isn't climbing—it's sprinting on flat ground. Nothing is in your way. Go!

ACTION ITEMS

There is no such thing as working too hard—not if you truly have a purpose and inspiration.

But there is such thing as sprinting too much without balance.

Rather than working yourself to death in a corporate environment like people did in the American Dream 1.0, practice meditation and mindfulness and finding inspiration from others.

I state it confidently that meditation is the single most important discovery I've made in my professional career. Yes, you read that correctly.

If a business owner would have said that in the American Dream 1.0? He would have been laughed out of the room.

But in the American Dream 2.0, it's a given that an important part of sprinting is rest.

With this rapidly changing environment come stronger mindsets, better attitudes, and a healthier body, which in turn make you more productive: "It's a marathon, not a sprint." Consistency is key, but just focus on the day. Win every day.

CHAPTER 6

* * *

BLAZING YOUR OWN TRAIL

By all means, you can start your career at an entry-level position.

Build some skills, and work your way up the ladder. It's admirable, and there are plenty of great job opportunities out there for people who are perfectly suited for those roles. As CEO, I have *incredible* talent who are my teammates in business. I pass zero judgment, and I've always tried to create an environment that allowed them to blossom and thrive, without the risk or stress of running their own show.

At some point, whether you work for someone and want to advance, or feel you might have developed enough of a skillset to branch out on your own, it's a wide-open landscape of opportunity for the risk-takers.

Some things to be mindful of:

- There is *no such thing* as security when it comes to work.

- Markets shift, and there is never a time or place where you are entirely secure.

- Corporations run P & Ls, and unfortunately your salary is a line item on them. Not always but sometimes. Overconfidence of job security is the ultimate exposure to future "life isn't fair" crying in your beer sob story.

Be the CEO of *you*, and own that role.

With all the opportunities available to you in the American Dream 2.0, you don't have to kiss ass anymore.

The only question now is, *"What is your story going to be?"*

And what an environment to share it!

- Film video content on your iPhone that empowers your brand and cost you nothing.
- Create your own YouTube channel.
- Set up a free blog on WordPress, and build an online community.
- Make business connections (aka virtual handshakes) that lead to real-life connections on social media, especially LinkedIn.

- Express an opinion to the world with a few lines on Twitter or a Facebook post.
- Show the images of your personal and professional life on Instagram.

People Google you. What do they find? Find your passion, and make your story.

Think about this: It truly is all about *your story*.

Let's look at the history of business.

Just like the Salad Bowl had a great story. The community loved the owners and talked about it. The owners had a great story, and it wasn't about salads; it was about culture and relationships.

The retailers crushed the mom-and-pops because they made things cheaper.

The internet came along and made things even quicker and cheaper than the retailers. Rest in peace, Blockbuster, Toys"R"Us, and any company that did not adapt.

Now there is social media.

We have come full circle. Your *story* matters now, more than ever. So I ask you again, "What is your story?"

Or some might call it your brand. I believe your brand is what people say about you, when you're not around. What are you known for?

It boils down to content and distribution. Create posts, videos, tweets, etc., *consistently*, and find distribution channels for that content to be seen. Content is king. Distribution is queen, and she wears the pants. Find your niche, build your story through content, and then grow your audience.

That's how you blaze your own trail.

ACTION ITEMS

Using social media, you have more B2B connectivity than ever before. Who do you want to build a relationship with?

Find your targets. Then ask them to be on your podcast, give a quote for your blog, or get interviewed for your YouTube channel. It's a click of the mouse to start the conversation.

Offer them something of value. You can easily get to know someone through clicking around online. Use that to find what's important to them. Maybe a charity?

Give. Give. Give *value*.

But start making connections.

CHAPTER 7

★ ★ ★

"YOUR INDUSTRY IS DYING"

I got into radio in 2009, just as it was taking its last gasps as a healthy industry.

It was a time of transition. The global economy had just crashed, this little phenomenon called YouTube was gaining prominence, social media was booming, and podcasting was on the upswing. If radio (and television) wanted to keep pace, they'd have to change.

But guess what? They didn't.

Fresh to the radio game, I wasn't tied to any traditions or old ways of thinking. I just got in front of the microphone and tried to bring value to people. I leveraged the show to build real relationships with thought leaders and influencers.

It wasn't until I attended a major media conference in Chicago that I got a glimpse of this industry's future. And it was ugly.

Now, on the surface, everything was fine and dandy. People were yukking it up at happy hours, shooting the shit at breakout sessions, and generally looking and feeling untouchable. These dinosaurs weren't aware of their soon-to-be extinction.

The vibe was exciting, but I was a fish out of water. I didn't know these people, and I was clueless when it came to radio and media. But my naivete would be my saving grace.

Most people think you have to be the smartest guy in the room or know the most people to succeed. When I went to this media conference, I was neither—and it made all the difference.

Bob Pittman, the founder of iHeartRadio and CEO of AOL, gave the keynote address. I sat in a massive auditorium with more than two thousand people, all hungover after nights of parties and happy hours.

He grabbed them all by the proverbial collar and pulled them all close with his predictions for the future of radio:

"We are working in a dying medium."

The thousands of people in the auditorium fell silent. It was like an entire industry had just been told by their doctor that they had only six months to live.

The old ways of radio no longer work. Selling advertising, pitching your show based on ratings—in five years, nobody will care. *Nobody* in this industry is adapting to that change, and it will kill you.

Your advertising revenue comes from the ROI you can provide advertisers. You show them the ratings, they pay you for ad space, and they get more return on their investment. The bad news: those methods have played out. The good news: radio is still the number one most engaging medium. People connect personally with radio more than anything else—even more than TV.

The only way you'll get that survive and thrive is through ROR: return on relationships—value you can offer your sponsors, beyond ROI, measured from ratings, and dollars and cents.

The people around me in the crowd whispered and scoffed at each other. I could feel them shuffling uncomfortably in their seats, refusing to accept what they'd just heard.

All the way up to that point at the conference, I'd felt out of place. But in that moment, I felt like Bob was speaking directly to me. I went from feeling like the dumbest guy in the room to being one of the few people who got what he was saying: the industry was moving, and nobody in that room was going to move with it. Here these people were resting on hope that someone would listen to their crappy shows, so they could sell off of ratings. I was looking at my show as the opportunity to leverage and build relationships.

To put that into perspective, I am now the CEO of a very successful media company and the host of a national TV show called *The American Dream* (check us out on Instagram: @theamericandreamtv). It all started with a radio show that *nobody* listened to.

And how did we grow? How did we get partners (sponsors) to spend money on a show *nobody* listened to?

ROR.

We found new ways to add *value* to our partners. For starters, we refer to the people we work with as partners, not advertisers, and we treat them as such. We learn about them as people, find out their goals and ambitions, and do what we can to help them reach those goals. We live by that old saying, "People don't care how much you know till they know how much you care."

At the Salad Bowl, my father ate lunch every day with his customers.

He cared.

I never miss an opportunity to sit down with someone. I've built a national TV show called *The American Dream* with a goal to win an Emmy—and I didn't do it hiding behind my computer. I flew around the country to meet our partners and build relationships with them.

What about you? What relationships do you build?

I love new-school technology, but the old school still wins on the relationship front.

Fast forward to now, and the radio industry has been crushed by podcasting. Radio as a singular medium is dead. The only ones who succeeded are the ones who evolved into multimediums.

Everyone in that industry thought they had it made. They didn't want to believe the changes happening, and they didn't realize they were dying a slow death as they romanticized about the way it used to be.

> *Good players go to the hockey puck; great players go to where the hockey puck is going to be.*
>
> —WAYNE GRETZKY

Bob Pittman told everyone in radio that the game was changing, and they still clutched to the past.

But dinosaurs don't want to be told they're dinosaurs.

ACTION ITEMS

I want you to look at your calendar for this coming month.

How many meetings do you have in the books?

- Coffee

- Breakfast

- Lunch

- Happy Hour

- Dinner

Five opportunities *a day* to break bread with someone and build relationships.

Remember, this is *your* American dream and nobody else's. *You* have to get it.

CHAPTER 8

* * *

CAN'T FIND OPPORTUNITIES? *CREATE THEM*

In 2008, there was a market crash.

Today, there is a technological tidal wave, and you can either drown in it or grab a surfboard and enjoy the ride.

That's what the CEO of VaynerMedia, Gary Vaynerchuk (or Gary Vee as most people call him), says.

Before he became one of the most successful podcasters and content creators in the world, Gary had a humble upbringing. After emigrating to the United States from the Soviet Union, his father built a liquor store in Springfield, New Jersey. Gary bagged ice for the liquor store through his childhood and adolescence.

Even as a young boy, he knew that bagging ice was not the wave of the future. He set his sights for something higher.

Despite being a C and D student throughout school, he graduated college. After he did, Gary took control of his father's liquor store, launched Wine Library, and had a daily webcast reviewing and recommending different types of wine.

Gary wasn't a world-class video editor or a brilliant scriptwriter. He was a guy with an idea and a Flip cam. So for one thousand straight days, he drank wine on camera, gave his honest reviews, and posted them online.

He didn't get worked up about making them perfect; he just took action and stuck with it.

Due in large part to the company's new online presence, he grew Wine Library from $3 million a year to $60 million.

Eventually, he parted ways with Wine Library (on good terms with his dad) and created VaynerMedia, which now has more than eight hundred employees and more than $100 million in annual revenue.

He's now one of the ultimate thought leaders in the digital world.

In 2018, I spent some time with Gary, and let me tell you something...

As the host of a national TV show, I've met some pretty big names. Hell, I worked for MTV in New York City where we had celebrities coming in and out of there every day. Nothing about celebrities impresses me, except the ones who work hard and have earned everything they have.

That is Gary Vee. He is a legitimate CEO who runs an incredible company with a terrific culture, and he wears his heart on his sleeve. He's one of the most authentic people you will ever meet—the real effing deal.

Don't know him?

Look him up and start following his podcast. If you take nothing else away from this book than discovering him, then your investment of time and money has been worthwhile. He's one of the best modern-day entrepreneurs on the planet. He curses like a sailor, but you can't knock his passion!

It doesn't matter where you come from or what your parents do for a living. In this country, if you have a vision for your future and you work hard to achieve it, anything is possible.

The American Dream 1.0, 2.0, 3.0, and beyond—that will never change.

ACTION ITEMS

At The American Dream TV, we look up to Gary Vee and his willingness to carve out a niche in the digital world. Gary shared with me that he has twenty-five people on his personal content team and is creating a hundred-plus pieces of content *a day*!

Regardless of the device or medium, it all comes down to great content. Good storytelling is always engaging, whether it's on TV, Facebook, or in your dad's liquor store, recorded on your crappy little Flip cam.

We love creating great content at The American Dream TV, and that content lives online. I'd love to hear from you on my Instagram page: @craigsewingmedia and @theamericandreamtv.

- What is your story?

- How much content do you create around it?

- Are you considered a thought leader in your space?

- What's stopping you?

PART 2

═══

AMERICAN DREAM 2.0 RELATIONSHIPS

CHAPTER 9

* * *

ROI VERSUS ROR

We've all heard of ROI: it's short for return on investment.

A business spends $X and wants to see a bigger $X + Y$ in return. Pretty simple.

Now, if you are on the *receiving end* of someone else's dollars, it's not just about ROI. You also need to deliver ROR, return on relationship. People neglect ROR all the time in business and in life. Expand the spectrum of value you provide.

Let's look at media as an example.

In the American Dream 1.0, companies paid a set amount of money for a specific number of ads, which resulted in a set number of views that ultimately led to a promised number of potential leads. That was a transactional, ROI-focused model. I call it a business on the "transaction treadmill."

That doesn't work in the American Dream 2.0.

And frankly, in my media company's early days, we couldn't offer potential partners any ROI—we didn't have "ratings" (another outdated American Dream 1.0 concept). Our show sucked, and nobody listened to it. We had to reinvent the wheel and create a paradigm shift to get that show sponsored. The tip of the arrow—the most important point—is this:

People want to be inspired and have a purpose.

In today's environment, it can be incredibly opportunistic to be a thought leader, which can be as simple as having a passion and sharing your vision. Mine was combatting negative media.

People really clung to that and still do. We were able to attract those who were like-minded. There was a real thirst for the positive message we represented.

If you have an inspirational message that people can get behind, you're already halfway there to giving people a valuable ROR. You are giving people a sense of purpose.

THE SEXINESS OF ROR

Preferably, you want people to invest in your idea because it's sexy; but sexiness wears off with time. It's about adding value.

There's nothing sexy about long hours and hard stretches of lean revenues. You don't want to have a revolving door of partners, no matter what form they come in.

You have to retain them. They have to see value, and if that value isn't in the ROI, show them the ROR. Sometimes it's connections. Sometimes it's your skillsets. Sometimes it's just your time. No matter what, though, your goal is to get them to buy in to you and your mission.

What are unique ways you can deliver value to someone? A partnership? A referral source?

When they value your relationship, they will devalue the importance of ROI.

ROI is one-dimensional, cold, and outdated.

ROR is multidimensional, inviting, and the key to business relationships of the future.

Now, I know you don't have a TV or radio show (but who's to say you couldn't). Still, the lesson is the same for you:

In business especially, if someone gives you their hard-earned dollar...

What value *are you providing them in return?*

We have a rule that for every dollar someone spends with us...

We want to give them 10x the value.

Spend a buck with us, we give you $10 in value.

Spend $1,000, we give you $10,000 in value.

Spend $10,000, we give you $100,000 in value.

It's our blueprint for success.

There's nothing I love more than a good whiteboard session with my team when we bring in a new partner. That's when we get to dollarize a new relationship and figure out exactly how we'll provide extra value to them.

We have an internal strategy session on all the things we can do to 10x the value for that partner.

And how do we learn this?

Um...we *talk to them!* Get to know them. Find out what their passions are and what's important to them. What are their short-term and long-term personal and professional goals?

We build real relationships with them. And most of all...

WE CARE.

ACTION ITEMS

Think about your friends, family, and business connections.

What ROR are you truly providing them?

To find success in the American Dream 2.0, it's all about adding value to others through relationships.

CHAPTER 10

***

10X THE VALUE

Back in my radio days, we experienced quite a bit of success. Later, this evolved to our TV show *The American Dream*, which I created in 2014 (@theamericandreamtv, www.americandreamnetwork.tv).

In the radio days, I became a consultant to other radio hosts across the country. You could call me a media coach—something I still do today. Even though I reference radio, truth is, it all falls under that modern-day buzzword of *content*. Today, podcasts are an even better medium, and you could start yours immediately for free!

You cannot gain market share without being a great marketer. That's done with content—specifically, video, digital, and social. Create engaging content!

As a media coach, I help people who try to take their show and business to the next level. They want bigger audiences and more clients. Simply put, they want to grow the footprint in their niche.

This is why most of them fail.

It's all about what *they* want, not what their audience wants. Too many businesses think about their objective first, without focusing on helping others accomplish theirs. It starts with thinking about the other person first and working your way backward.

Reverse engineer the value.

Valerie Geller, who wrote the book *Creating Powerful Radio*, had three rules about content that I love:

1. Tell the truth.
2. Make it matter.
3. Never be boring.

For most people, it's number 2 that goes over their head. Nobody asks themselves the question:

Why on earth should anyone listen to me?

Whether it's blogs, podcasts, Facebook posts, YouTube

videos, Instagram stories, Facebook Live, or even just a face-to-face conversation,

CONTENT IS KING.

Content is free to produce these days.

When you talk about ROI versus ROR, now you're talking about people spending their money with you and generating an income stream.

I remember one very specific coaching call with a radio host in a different city, where they "lost another one," aka a sponsor for their show, and wanted my advice.

The conversation went like this:

Host: "I have this awesome show, but I can't keep a partner."

Me: "Your show sucks."

Host: "Huh?"

Me: "Have you actually listened to it? It's just not very good.

"It's all about you pontificating how much smarter you are than everyone else in the world, rather than adding value to the end-all listener.

"And truth is, you're a shitty partner. You do nothing to add value to your partners besides praying that someone reaches out to them. What have you done for your partners this past month?"

Host: [Silent]

We then created a game plan.

We had to crush the ROI paradigm and create a shift, one where his partners saw ROR.

In the ROI model, those partners spent money hoping someone listened to their crappy show and would magically call to give their business. In today's environment, maybe it's a YouTube channel, podcast, or Facebook strategy.

In the ROR model, those partners spent money, and he made it crystal clear he'd deliver 10x the value of their investment. In doing so, he created 10x value for his partners.

Here are just a few of the initiatives we implemented:

- Weekly coaching calls, where he got to understand his partners' businesses better
- Monthly meetings and strategy sessions

- Introduction to other professionals (networking)
- Business events and masterminding
- Creating content and allowing sponsors to make updates on the show
- Sending that content to his partners for their repurposing
- Created marketing collateral that his partners could use for their marketing
- Social media endorsements

And the list went on and on.

See what I mean? 10x the value.

You can't just think you're some brilliant thought leader and assume that's going to monetize. You might be smart, but that's just dumb.

The point is, find ways to *add value*.

We *squashed* the ROI equation and made it all about ROR. And we can tailor this conversation a little bit differently. Maybe you aren't trying to attract sponsors into your model, but you do want to have more customers or clients. The same goes for you.

What value are you giving to the end-all user?

That's the whole point. Return on relationship could simply mean what kind of relational equity you build through providing value to someone.

CHAPTER 11

* * *

PARTNERS, NOT ADVERTISERS

Our national TV Show *The American Dream* (Facebook. com/theamericandreamtv) doesn't have advertisers—we have partners. This is just how we happen to work. Hopefully, it's relatable. Many, or most, businesses somehow, in some way, have some form of partnership.

Advertisers are an American Dream 1.0 concept. They're faceless, nameless entities floating out there. If you want to know why the mainstream produces garbage, it's because the sheeple watch it or click on it. Advertisers like that.

The Kardashians, Honey Boo Boo, *all* of MTV, the 24/7 news...

It's all garbage. Clicks = dollars. That's crap, and why most have cut the cord for cable and don't watch the news.

Our media game has always stood for something and combatted this clutter. And because of this, as we've grown in our model, we create partnerships around real relationships. It's a different mode in this space. But this can be true for many spaces, no matter your industry.

How do you align relationships as partners for a greater good? One of value, integrity, and purpose.

Partners are people you meet for a beer and fly around the country to visit face-to-face and develop a relationship with. They're friends who work with you to build something together, people you've vetted and share a common desire. It's not always easy to find, but when you do, you nurture these relationships.

On *The American Dream*, we combat negative media through positive and inspiring stories.

It's working—both B2C (people who watch) and B2B (businesses that align with us).

We have a common cause. It's really that simple. Some might call it a brand.

What is your cause? What is your brand?

In our space, people are sick and tired of the political divide, the negative nonsense, and the Kardashian pop culture, so we hit them with stories that unite.

We partner with people who share that passion with us, and it makes us more successful in the process. We collectively want to make an impact, and it tends to be the commonality of our story.

Look at your own business.

Are you flying solo?

Creating key relationships?

Are those relationships truly partners or just convenient alignments?

The former is where growth comes from.

ACTION ITEMS

Nobody watched our show at first, but we continued to create positive and engaging content. We didn't have ratings to sell to sponsors; we had a message in *The American Dream* that we *shared* with them. It connected.

By allowing people to be partners, we allowed them to leverage the platform we'd created.

How can you create value for your *partners*? What do your ideal partnerships look like? Who do you know that might be able to connect you in some way, shape, or form?

Perhaps just family and friends and the relationships that mean the most.

How can you add value to others?

Always start there!

CHAPTER 12

★ ★ ★

YOU NEED A "BRAND-AID"

Not much speaks to the American dream more than the concept of homeownership, even if you're not in the real estate business. Hard to deny this one. Maybe you own a home or plan to at some point. There's something special about owning a piece of land that you reside on. Maybe just pride, if nothing else. But ultimately, you need food, you need water, you need shelter. That last one is what we call home.

Today, technology has changed the game of house hunting pretty dramatically. Kind of a fascinating space actually. Always has been and always will be.

Most home searches start with a Google search or Zillow. This could change even by the time this book comes out.

You click the links and find a list of homes that fit the framework of what you're looking for. The first one you find has more than twenty professional pictures. The location is right next to work, it's in a nice school district, and the lawn has just the right amount of space for your dogs to play.

It's your American dream. On this topic at least.

You want more information, so you fill out the contact form on the right, directly underneath the random Realtor you've never seen before in your life.

That's just the agent who has that listing, right? It's just luck of the draw that the owner chose to use their services.

Actually, that's not the case. That Realtor actually *paid* Zillow to have their picture put there with the listing. Sadly, many real estate agents refer to this as "marketing." Many industries work this exact way. One million–pound gorilla aggregates a lot of attention. That million-pound gorilla sells that to those who can't do it on their own.

Truth be told, funding someone else's company by purchasing leads is not marketing—not for any industry. Nothing against Zillow. They've mastered the game of technology. And it's "the people" who determine the value of a platform, not me. Clearly, they know their way in this space.

As for Realtors in this example, in any city there are, on average, fifteen thousand Realtors. It's the most saturated profession in the world. It takes longer to get your hairstyling license than it does to get your real estate license. This industry is, and always will be, the most interesting to keep an eye on in the American Dream 2.0.

Realtors, aka commission salespeople, facilitate your biggest investment—the place where you'll create tax advantages, build equity, and gain financial stability. But it's more than this; it's a place where you'll live, build memories, and grow neighborhoods.

It's more than just an investment; it's your *home*.

It's not the kind of purchase that should be reached by shortcuts, but that's what so many professionals do in so many important professions: just buy leads. It's the American Dream 2.0 gone stupid—the transactional treadmill, the uneducated consumer loses.

In any business, not just real estate, if you're just buying your leads, you're doomed for failure. You're basically making the statement, "It's better to build someone else's brand than your own."

Stop building another company's brand; build your own relationships.

ACTION ITEMS

Gary Vaynerchuk once brilliantly urged Realtors to "be the digital mayor of your market."

In an American Dream 2.0 kinda world, people should go to you, not the local newspaper, for information within your industry or rippling closely enough. What content positions you as that digital mayor?

CHAPTER 13

* * *

THERE'S NO "I" IN TEAM

We learn from failures, so I don't mind sharing one of my biggest ones with you.

Many years ago, I organized a big B2B event in San Diego for other professionals looking to step up their business game. There were thousands of attendees, and the event was a huge success. None of it would have been possible without the partners of the event, those who contributed financially in sponsorship.

When it finished, I was beyond fired up as thousands of people filled the streets and entered the downtown bars and restaurants. We had just done a cannonball into the market, and the ripple effect was *big*.

In a moment of euphoria, I sent a mass thank-you email to all of the attendees. In it, I said something to the effects of, "Thank you for coming to the event, was an honor to put it on, blah blah blah."

Seemed harmless enough, right?

Wrong.

While the email was a token of my appreciation to everyone who attended, it inadvertently insulted a sponsor of the event for not being recognized. This sponsor was the financial backbone of the event. I took ownership of something, that if it wasn't for the help of others, the event would have never been possible.

The next week, I went to lunch with the owner of the company who was offended—not just an owner but also a friend of mine. He said he "needed to talk to me."

We rode together to grab some lunch.

We pulled into the restaurant parking lot and the conversation started. We just sat idle and never even made it to lunch.

The conversation started like this.

Owner: "Man, we put a lot of money and hard work into that event...We had tons of people from our team cheering it on and helping put it together to drive attendees. In your follow-up email, you didn't even acknowledge us."

Granted, my friend knew I had good intentions and where my heart was at. This was more like when you were growing up, and your mom said, "I'm not mad. I'm disappointed." Everyone knows that the latter stings way worse!

He did understand—it was an innocent mistake.

However, as the leader of his company, he was a voice for the voiceless—those people in his company who would have loved the acknowledgment. I got so caught up in the moment that I didn't acknowledge the people who deserved it. Those who put a stake on my name, who endorsed me.

There are few sentences more painful to hear from the mouth of a grown man than "you let me down." But that's what I'd done.

It crushed me.

While I'd never meant anything malicious by the omission, and was just caught up in the excitement of the event's success, I still royally screwed up—with something as simple as sending a thank-you email.

You can run fast on your own, but you can go *far* with others.

You are not going to get anywhere alone.

Even if you're working your ass off, hustling, grinding, innovating, building, and deserve a whole lot of credit, others will be a part of your success.

Make it a habit every day to recognize those around you and be grateful for them. Who on your team, in your sphere, or maybe just an acquaintance on Facebook deserves some acknowledgment?

Relationships are the single most important ingredient, even in an American Dream 2.0 kinda world. Never underestimate the importance of something as simple as saying, "Thank you."

Burn the word *I*.

Get good at using the word *we*.

ACTION ITEMS

One of the strongest words in the English language is *we*. Practice using it more habitually.

Some people are meant to be leaders; some people aren't. It does get lonely at the top, but you wouldn't get there without others. If you choose to be that leader, don't forget your teammates along the way.

This book is about building true relationships and being a servant leader. In the American dream, it's much more respected than the outdated term of *boss*.

Those who command respect don't demand it.

CHAPTER 14

★ ★ ★

THE VALUE OF
A CHEERS

They say your "network is your net worth."

But how do we even measure that anymore?

In the American Dream 2.0 landscape, your network can be *huge*. But let's not forget the values of the 1.0 days, where networking meant building social capital—shaking hands.

The digital space, social media, funnels, geotargeting, email campaigns—all the latest buzzwords allow you to cast a wide net and help you find some connectivity at your fingertips. But real relationships are built in person. You grab a coffee or drink a beer with people, in person, not through laptops.

HIDING BEHIND YOUR COMPUTER

Too many entrepreneurs (many just wantrepreneurs) hide behind their computers doing webinars and creating bullshit sales funnels. That's not to say these are all bad. Some are fine, but you cannot substitute them for real relationships.

An email can't shake a hand or give a hug.

Sometimes I think people in the American Dream 1.0 had an advantage without computers. They had no choice but to build relationships in person.

Here's how important relationships are to me: I fly all over the country to meet with potential guests and partners of my show, *The American Dream TV* (follow us on Instagram: @theamericandreamtv and @craigsewingmedia). I built an entire national show, one city and one person at a time, living out of a suitcase, in hotel rooms, as I met with people for lunch, dinner, drinks, and coffee.

For the better part of a year, had you joined one of my meetings regarding our show launching in that market, you could've stuck around after everyone left and you would have seen me lying on the floor of the conference room.

Hustling the country like this caused massive back pains. But there is no substitution for being face-to-face with your partnerships.

I once even flew into Phoenix to cheers *one* beer.

I was about to leave the country for a couple of weeks when I got an email:

"Craig, we'd love it if you could come to Phoenix. It would mean so much to the people here who support the show." Of course, I talk about the show, but stories like this can easily be translated to your profession—same but different.

I had every excuse in the book to skip it: I was on my way out of the country, and it's not like this partner would drop us if I didn't stop at this happy hour event.

But I made the choice long ago to prioritize relationships over everything else. So I stopped in Phoenix on my way out, and I stayed long enough for exactly one beer. Beer in one hand, luggage in the other.

And you know something?

It was totally worth it. Things like that don't go unnoticed.

That's ROR.

When you have opportunities to show people how much you care, don't look at the measurable ROI; instead, look at the incalculable ROR. The old saying goes, "People don't care how much you know till they know how much you care."

That was true for the American Dream 1.0, and it's true in the American Dream 2.0 as well.

So much of the world is automating. People think an email is the same as a phone call. It's not, and neither compares to spending time with someone. It's almost becoming a long-lost art. Those succeeding in the American Dream 2.0 will make this 1.0 core value a mandatory standard.

Businesses focus on sales funnels, drip campaigns, social media spam, and creating bots. While everyone goes that way, consider going the other way.

Double down on human beings.

ACTION ITEMS

You should never eat alone. All three meals, *plus* coffee and happy hour, are an opportunity for a connection.

5x opportunities per day.

25x per workweek.

That equals 100x opportunities per month!

Eating out with business connections might sound expensive, but look at it like this. Let's say you spend $2,000 on one hundred meetings with business contacts. Those hundred connections will undoubtedly create enough opportunities to more than make up for the $2,000 you spent on those meetings.

CHAPTER 15

* * *

THE ART OF CONNECTION

Some call it networking; I call it building social capital. In the American Dream 1.0, it was possible to succeed as a one-dimensional business. You sold shoes? Great, you focused on that. People need shoes. Find more feet to put them on.

But with the American Dream 2.0?

You need to be more well-rounded. The product is important, but so is the story around the brand. That story isn't just one of the neighborhood; it lives online. It's an online network. But whether it's real people networking or online connecting, having a story and knowing the story of others has a tremendous amount of value.

It allows you to be a magnet for connection and also a force for it. It can work synergistically.

We'll stick with the real estate example, since it's relatable. A home purchase is such an important facet of the American dream, 1.0 or 2.0. And for us, the American dream is a show the shares the stories of our cities, via lifestyle, culture, and real estate. Very much in our wheelhouse!

Imagine you're a real estate agent. Essentially a 1099 contractor. No base pay. One hundred percent commission. What you kill is what you eat. When someone buys a house, they need a mortgage.

Do you have a mortgage professional you can refer them to?

They will get tax write-offs on the mortgage interest.

Do you know a CPA they can contact?

They might have to pull money out of accounts to put down a down payment.

Do you know a financial advisor?

After they own the home, they might want to pass it down to their children.

Do you know someone who can help them draft a will and an estate plan?

By building a network of professionals, you become much more valuable than if you were a one-dimensional operator, floating in space all by yourself. Be the hub of your business wheel. Who are the spokes you could align with? In doing so, you can also become a spoke on theirs.

The value in one client is far beyond just that one transaction. Not to mention, treat that client well, that'll snowball into more referrals, which is what most in these types of positions want. Connectivity has exponential value.

That's return on relationship. That's how you build "leads" in the American Dream 2.0. Just get referred! It kills me how many professionals *buy leads* for their business. *Buy leads?* That is no business; that is a transactional treadmill. There is no equity in the business model.

You are only as good as your last deal. Relationships refer.

You don't buy them; you earn them.

PART 3

═══

AMERICAN DREAM 2.0 MINDSET

CHAPTER 16

* * *

GIVE TO RECEIVE

You can connect with anyone in the world with the click of a mouse. Never has there been such a time to scale! As a result, you have more opportunities to give value than ever before.

This content game is real, but just like the American Dream 1.0, when you're building relationships in person, giving is always the first step in receiving.

So much online content is *me, me, me, I do this, I do that.* I'm an expert in [fill in the blank]. Or even worse, I think I'm hot, look at this selfie, give me some likes, thanks. So many people have to tell you what an expert they are rather than just *being one.*

Whether you're posting online or getting to know someone face-to-face, your goal should be to breathe oxygen into *their* success. What value are you providing to the person on the other end?

In 2019, we put on a conference for our American Dream partners, American Dream 1.0 style—face-to-face. Not just some webinar, even though that is *much* easier. Sam Kohramian, CEO of Big Block Realty, number 37 Inc 500 fastest-growing companies, took the stage and got a nice laugh out of our audience.

He stated to the audience, "Sewing asked me to speak here today...So I text him, 'What topic do you want me to speak about?' He responded, 'ADD VALUE.' I was like, what the hell... Okay. So I responded with a bunch of topics for him to consider. He said, 'ADD VALUE.' That's all this guy said in my texts. So, um, here I am... Want some value?"

Sam K then fired home with knowledge, ended up *crushing* his presentation, and had the audience's head spinning with new knowledge they didn't have before that presentation.

I walked out to the stage with a handheld mic, and we collectively dropped it in front of everyone. #micdrop.

But here's the point: At this event, two days start to finish— as a team coordinating this event—our mantra was *value*.

We had no selling from stage and no vendors spoke from stage. We crammed in more than thirty speakers, lightning round style...and it was *all value*.

Then we finished with a happy hour, building relationships American Dream 1.0 style. At the end, we were told many times over, "This was the best conference I've ever been to."

Maybe it was, or maybe they had too many cocktails, but those two things can go hand in hand. Sometimes just having a good time is all the value people need.

An interesting point about that event...

Despite having ticket prices at $500 a pop and sponsoring partners, we *lost* money on the event, had to come out of pocket. So we weren't just adding value to our attendees; we were even investing in it!

> In an online world, are you still getting out there face-to-face? Building real relationships? This is being lost in today's 2.0 world, and it's more effective than anything you will ever do online.
>
> Trade webinars, and do seminars. Use webinars to drive people to your seminars or events.
>
> Is it more difficult? Yes.
>
> Is it riskier? Yes. But the rewards are bigger. Get out, and do events! I don't care if it's a lunch 'n' learn with five people. *Nothing* beats face-to-face. At the Salad Bowl, David Sewing ate with his customers almost every single day!

Grant Cardone, the best-selling author and sales trainer whose motto is "10x Your Business," is a polarizing character. He epitomizes the American Dream 2.0.

Grant is a frequent guest on *The American Dream TV*, and here's what I can say with absolute certainty: whether you like Grant or not, he definitely puts in the work. Talk is cheap, but he walks the walk. And I don't care what you think about him, that's admirable.

Personally, I believe Grant Cardone is a great illustration of someone winning with the American Dream 2.0. He gets that it's all about working hard and still having old-school hustle. He just happens to leverage the hell out of social media. Follow this guy on Instagram; he's a riot. You might love him or hate him, but he hustles.

In 2018, I met with Grant in his Miami office, a building he owned.

He's a little more "all about the money" than me in his brand, but whatever.

To each his own. Just not my thing.

Grant and I in 2019. Quite the motivational quote walking into his office. A little blunt. But seriously, the American Dream has no room for whiners, and a little kick in the butt motivation never hurt anyone.

When I walked onto his sales floor, I was met with an entire office of people standing on their feet, clapping their hands and shouting, "What's up, Craig?" You can find the video somewhere on my Instagram page @ craigsewingmedia somewhere in 2018.

Talk about hospitality. His value to his customers is giving them guidance to 10x their business—more specifically, their goals.

> What are your goals? Write them down. Just for the hell of it, take it x10. What does that look like? It's okay to have ridiculous goals. Recently, I posted on Facebook, "Nobody should believe your goals except you." What are your goals?
>
> Try writing them out and taking it x10!
>
> See how that looks.

One of the best ways to bring value to other people is through connection—specifically, connecting them to other people. Your skillset is limited, but as Bob Beaudine writes in *The Power of Who*, who do ya know?

With every person you meet, ask yourself:

Who do I know who could help this person?

Who do I know who this person could help?

You don't even have to have the right advice; just be the connector. (This is where your network becomes your net worth.)

And then there's you.

What can you *teach* people? How can you add value to someone's life?

You have gifts, talents, experiences, knowledge, and skills. How can you provide them to one person? Or in the world of the American Dream 2.0, how can you unleash them to the masses?

How in 2.0?

1. Email campaigns
2. Blogs
3. Social media posts—on all the outlets
4. Newsletters
5. Video
6. Live streams
7. Webinars
8. YouTube and Vimeo content

***And *please* don't forget, there is still something incredibly valuable about *in person.*

1. Events
2. Lunch 'n' learns
3. Seminars
4. Conferences
5. Coffee appointments
6. Grabbing a beer

No matter how you do it, content is king, and your unique knowledge and experience will drive the content you create. Give it to the universe. The universe will find ways to reward you.

Not everything needs a price tag.

Share your value with no expectation.

WHAT IF PEOPLE COPY MY CONTENT?

My mantra is, "The moment I *stop* getting copied is the moment I have a problem."

Truth is, you could give your competition the playbook; if you're legit, they would never execute on your level.

Copying is the best compliment mediocracy can give to greatness.

THE AMERICAN DREAM, AS
DEFINED BY GRANT CARDONE

The definition of the American dream is, the idea that every US citizen should have an equal opportunity to achieve success and prosperity through hard work, determination, and initiative.

The American dream, to me, is the possibility for all to have success. The bigger issue is how people define success.

For me, the ultimate American dream is the possibility for every person to have true freedom to live where they want, do what they want, practice their beliefs without interference, and to do so as long as they want with whomever they want.

I am living proof that the American dream is possible. I had no money, no connections, no handouts, and no assistance from Wall Street or some lucky streak. But instead, through hard work, discipline, good decision making, and persistence, I was able to get myself into a position to provide my family with almost anything they need and want.

2019 picture with Grant Cardone in Miami at his private jet. Some aspire for things like private jets, some aspire for less material things. Whatever YOU aspire for, 10x your thinking about it. That's American Dream 2.0 thinking!

CHAPTER 17

★ ★ ★

NINETY-NINE PROBLEMS, BUT A CONNECTION AIN'T ONE

As mentioned earlier, Bob Beaudine (author of *The Power of Who*) was *Sports Illustrated* "Most important man in sports that nobody knows."

Bob doesn't strike out batters or hit three-pointers. He doesn't run a front office either. Bob's known for connecting coaches with teams, a cool kinda sports head hunter.

Talk about a fun job!

But I got to know and love Bob, because of his bestseller,

The Power of Who, his book detailing his life work and philosophy of connecting people with people. Bob understands the power of *who*, as in, who do you know?

This is a powerful thing in the American Dream 1.0, with real relationships, as well as in 2.0, with online connectivity.

The truth is, everybody already knows everyone they need to know. The only problem is that most people don't let anyone know what they need, so nobody can help even if they want to.

Think about a time when you've struggled with someone, maybe you lost your job. For some reason, we tend to shell up and not ask for help or connection.

Now let's flip the script. If someone you cared about came to you and said they needed some help, wouldn't you have been glad to make a connection?

Of course you would.

That's what friends are for, so don't rob someone of the opportunity to do the same for you. The people who care about you are the most well equipped to help you.

For many people, it's a pride issue.

They just don't want to tell anyone that they lost their job, that they're lonely and single, or that they want to start a new career. So they stay unemployed, they don't find a partner, or they get stuck in careers they hate.

Bob Beaudine realized that you have to open up about your adversity to allow your network to help you. If you keep everything inside, nobody can help you. Are you guilty of this? When you need help, ask for it.

But here is the best way to illustrate the point.

If a good friend needed something from you, wouldn't you *want* to help them? Doesn't it feel good to *give* the gift on Christmas (or whatever holiday), rather than receive one?

Some of this stuff might feel a little basic.

But truth is, Bob Beaudine nailed it. The real message here is being a connector.

As far as I'm concerned, we live in a world where a résumé is as worthless as the paper it's written on. You won't find your American dream with a résumé posted on Monster. com; you'll find your path through connections.

I don't care how many problems you have; they can all be solved through relationships and connectivity.

- Now take a quick moment and write down twenty people you know, love, and trust.

- Put a star next to five of them.

- Circle one.

How could the people you know, love, and trust be the connection you need to advance some portion of your life?

Give them that opportunity. And if nothing else, maybe just reach out to them and see what they might need from you.

CHAPTER 18

DON'T BE "THAT GUY"

You've seen it countless times now, the "sign up and pay me for my webinar to learn how to make money getting people to pay for your webinars."

The modern-day snake oil salesperson.

Or how about this one: "Sign up to learn how to get ten thousand Instagram followers."

Vomit worthy.

But whatever.

If you can't sniff out that bullshit, I can't help you.

But let's dive a little deeper into the mistakes I see great people making, who have good intentions with their business or passion. The ones who heard that Facebook is a great place to be a marketer. All in all, that's pretty innocent. Facebook is quite possibly the best marketing medium in the history of life.

But that's just the platform.

What you do with it is what matters. You could give a five-year-old an AK-47 and give the same gun to a marine. You're going to have very different results. Where so many get it wrong is the content. Flooding people's feeds with content and just direct call to actions—"Call me. I'm the best at XYZ"—is so incredibly counterproductive.

Gary Vaynerchuk in *Jab Jab Jab Hook* is one of the best books on blending quality content with call to actions. Just like a good boxer, you must lead with jabs before you go for the hook. Too many people and businesses are just throwing haymakers, looking for the knockout punch.

That's about as much "game" as a drunk ass at a bar skipping asking for a number, and to go on a date, and rather going straight to "let's have sex." Good luck with that strategy.

As Rick James, or actually Dave Chapelle's version of him, once said, "What did five fingers say to the face? SMACK!"

Truth is, too many businesses have no patience with their marketing. They go straight to the call to action but have delivered no value leading up to it. Just like the American Dream 1.0, in the American Dream 2.0, there are no shortcuts. But that's marketing. You can't gain market share without being a great marketer. It can be the most fun part of business. Just gotta be patient and consistent.

It takes time for things to develop. If you are one-dimensional or so eager you can't take time to build brand equity, and just blast people with "call to actions," you'll get shot down like that drunk guy at the bar.

ACTION ITEMS

In this vast world of social media, I *love* Facebook group pages. It takes this massive ecosystem (like Facebook) and brings in a little more personal connectivity. Whether you join groups or, better yet, start your own, you are building your own community within the community.

For example, start a neighborhood group page where you invite people from your community. Perhaps you served in the military, you like sports, or reading books. Create pages for those communities. Once created, add value by delivering meaningful content into it. This is such a great way to build a referral network. It breaks down the quantity of social media into quality connection.

Make this a place that your community enjoys the content you share and keeps coming back. It's a unique way to be a leader in the American Dream 2.0, and *anyone* can do it.

CHAPTER 19

★ ★ ★

KICK FEAR IN
THE FACE

Mikey was a radio host.

He gave the best endorsements you ever heard on his shows.

If he was sponsored by a mattress company, he raved about the softest, most comfortable mattress he'd ever used. If it was a restaurant, he gave you all the details about his amazing experience eating dinner there. It was authentic and passionate.

The man was honest and enthusiastic. Despite being a radio show host and the fact that you were only hearing him, he had a unique way of getting you to also *see* what he was saying.

I enjoyed his show, but I *really* enjoyed the authenticity of how he endorsed.

In 2007, I owned a mortgage company. I was proud of our business and how we helped families finance the American dream of homeownership. I had to get him to endorse my mortgage company. This was long before I ever started a media company.

I picked up the phone the old-fashioned way and called the station looking for Mikey. Somehow, I got through and we set up a meeting. It was in a sharp-looking conference room at the station. Some cool art all over the walls, signed guitars, pictures of bands who'd been in the studio—the stereotypical rock 'n' roll look.

But those were the old days when there used to be real music and when MTV actually played music videos, not this reality garbage channel they've turned into. In 2001 when I lived in New York City and worked for MTV, the story was quite a bit different. That network went rotten quickly.

Sorry, I digress.

As for the *Mikey Show*, they put us through the sales process, pretended that they had to "approve" our endorsement. I told them all of our accolades, explaining that we were the top-rated company nationally, and they listened politely.

In reality, they would have taken our money no matter what, but my business partner and I didn't know anything about radio. Long story short, we got approved. We were invited back to sign on an agreement by a sales guy named Brian, a young guy, couldn't have been more than twenty-four years old.

He flipped through our agreement until he came to the final page. He looked up with what seemed like an authentic idea.

"You know, for the money you're about to spend advertising on the *Mikey Show*, you could just have *your own show*."

My partner and I looked at each other. "What are you talking about?"

"Your ad space with Mikey costs $3,600 per month. That's the same price it costs to buy your own weekend time slot."

"Seriously? What time of day?"

"Seven in the morning on Sundays, on the sports channel."

It didn't even occur to me how stupid it was: *Are we really*

about to pay money to do a talk show on the sports channel...
at 7:00 a.m. live *on Sundays?*

Yeah, well, we weren't that smart. We said yes.

In fact, I think it was more of a HELL YEAH!

Looking back on it, we were incredibly naive. We had no business hosting a show. At the time, I feared public speaking, and our subject matter didn't even fit the channel.

But despite all that, we did it.

As CEO Cody Barbo, tech guru, once said on our show *The American Dream*, "Sometimes you just gotta kick fear in the face." (I think we made a meme about it and posted it on my Instagram handle @craigsewingmedia.)

I didn't expect to find that opportunity when I walked into the radio station that day, but I found it. The universe presents you opportunities you don't always expect. I owed it to my American dream to take that risk. While I had *zero* skills in hosting a show, the one skill I owned was an unwillingness to let fear stop my ambitions. Growth comes from discomfort.

This was the beginning of my media career. Aside from

working at MTV in New York City at age twenty-one, I was clueless to this space but eager to do some trailblazing.

This was the inception of what ultimately led me to being the CEO of a media company with an amazing team, content spread across the country, thousands of supporters, now millions in annual sponsorship. Most importantly, crushing the initial fears and now taking the stage public speaking every week with a passion and a purpose.

I say none of that to brag; it's just hard not to pinch myself sometimes knowing what could have paralyzed the dream was just an obstacle that ambition allowed us to steamroll.

Kick fear in the face!

ACTION ITEMS

Truth is, growth comes from discomfort.

Opportunities always surface in the places where you're most afraid. If you know it's good for you, *take action*.

What opportunity do you *know* exists for you right now?

You know what I'm talking about, the one you keep procrastinating on, likely because of some form of fear. Be honest with yourself. Take a pen and write it down. *Why?* Write down *the worst* that can happen. Is it *really* that bad? Probably not.

Is it a video blog?

Starting that podcast?

Reaching out to that one person you know you want to meet?

Get out there and *fail forward* and kick fear in the face.

That's the only way to grow.

CHAPTER 20

★ ★ ★

AND BE WILLING TO GET KICKED IN THE FACE

I love Muay Thai boxing. It's meditative to break a sweat as my gloves and shins smack against the kicking pads. For years, I trained just for stress relief and exercise. Some people like to do crossword puzzles; I for some reason like to kick shit.

There's something about a sport where it's *all on you* with no teammates—you win alone, you lose alone. Even so, I wasn't competitive in it; I just enjoyed the thrill.

So there I was, on a vacation in Thailand with a small group of friends, where Muay Thai kickboxing originated. We made our way to a beautiful island called Phi Phi. If you've never gone, please make it a bucket list item. It's somewhere everyone needs to visit before the day they die. Great scenery, great people, therapeutic.

We were walking through a beach neighborhood, enjoying the sunset and doing what vacationers do: drinking. Suddenly, we caught sight of a Muay Thai boxing ring in the middle of one of the bars. Little did I know this would lead to one of the most important moments of my life.

It looked interesting. A Thai kickboxing ring in a venue that sold alcohol? Seemed like a good enough idea, and we decided to go check this thing out. We were disappointed to see that the ring was empty. Then we noticed several Thai men walking around carrying signs stating:

"Fight and get a free bucket of beer."

Suddenly, a little white guy with black hair and wearing boxing shorts got into the ring and started taunting the crowd, trying to bait people into fighting. Seemed incredibly overconfident. Apparently, his confidence was discouraging to the crowd, because nobody took him up on the offer to fight.

I honestly don't really remember the thought process, but I stood up. "Screw it. I'll fight." Call it liquid courage, I guess.

Within thirty seconds, two Thai guys had me undressed and in Thai boxing shorts, strapping up my hands with gloves. Within two minutes of standing up, I was in the ring, geared up and ready to go.

This was Thailand, mind you. There was no paperwork, no disclaimers, and no signatures. Also, no doctors on site and no ambulances, in case you took a shin to the grill. This was *old school* (call it the Thai Dream 1.0).

I looked at my friends as I stretched. I'll never forget the looks on their faces: *shocked*.

Just as I felt my confidence overflowing, the pip-squeak was gone, and I looked across the ring to find a *beast* in his place—a British guy, weighed about 275 pounds, and had a cinder block on his neck you would refer to as his head.

This is not what I signed up for. But then again, there was no sign-in sheet.

Hmm...Okay, well, apparently a bait and switch, or perhaps I just wasn't paying attention. Either way, no backing down now. As Tony Robbins puts it, "Can't take the island without burning the boats." Things just got really, really *real* in that ring.

Before I knew what was happening, we were touching gloves, going back to our corners, and there it was...*Ding! Ding! Ding!*

Round 1 was full of wild haymakers from both of us. I landed huge shots, but I swear this guy's head had nothing in it to damage. Punch after punch, I ran him into the ropes and gave it everything I had. This wasn't some fun sparring match in a gym in the United States. This was an all-about brawl. I was making solid connections with both left and right, but when you're punching a cinder block, it takes a bit more than one knockout punch.

Round 1 ended. I won that round, but I was already gassed. Did I mention I'd been drinking before this?

Round 2, he got smart. Realizing he outweighed me, I spent much of the round getting tackled onto my back. He put his head down like an enraged bull and just charged forward.

That's not exactly a legal move in Thai boxing, but this wasn't exactly a regulated fight. All the while, the crowd seemed to enjoy the chaos.

Round 3 finished with a slugfest. Blow after blow, we both put it all out there to the point of exhaustion.

Ding! Ding! Ding!

Just like that, the fight was over, and so was my Muay Thai boxing career, finishing with a 1–0 record. We both got our hands raised for a lively and appreciative crowd, but I'm taking that win with me, at least into my own book. If that blockhead ever writes a book, he can make up whatever story he wants with no judgment from me. But I kicked his ass. More importantly, I kicked fear in the face again.

The ref didn't hand me a championship belt or a trophy, but I did get that free bucket of beer. Good enough. But before I could even *think* about drinking another, I ran to the bathroom to wipe my face. In the mirror, I could already see the deep purple of a bruise working its way from my chest down my arm. I'd find out once I got back to the States that it was a torn pec. I didn't notice during the fight, which I find to be incredible given the nature of the injury, but that's what happens when you are in a moment like that.

Both the smell of the bathroom and the exhaustion overwhelmed me. Let me tell you, this wasn't exactly a five-star hotel. Imagine the smell of a concrete Thai bathroom with crappy plumbing (pun intended).

I puked in the sink before going back out to my friends.

Wouldn't you know it, they already drank all the beer with the group that was there supporting the British guy I fought.

What came out of that experience was something that will live with me forever: putting myself in a pretty dangerous situation in the spirit of overcoming a fear.

The fear, the anxiety, the risk—in most cases, we run from those things, but at that moment I hit it head-on. I would equate it to those who love jumping out of airplanes. Something about that rush has a ripple effect into your life. Now, this doesn't mean you have to do either of those activities, but can you at least imagine how taking a big risk can have other benefits?

Let's make this relatable to your American Dream 2.0.

Maybe it's as simple as setting up that high-level meeting, doing your first video for marketing, or a Facebook live. Or perhaps putting yourself in a position to speak publicly. Hell, maybe just standing up for yourself to your boss or spouse!

Confidence and self-respect aren't necessarily things we are born with. We have to prove it to ourselves. Only *you* can determine where your growth can come from.

As for me, whenever I'm on stage or doing something that makes me nervous, I think back to that moment—when I turned around and saw a massive dude in the ring. I had every excuse in the book to run away.

But I didn't.

What I got in return was one of the best moments of my life, where I overcame an insane amount of fear. Moving forward, I can take risks knowing that the worst that can happen is not nearly what that could've been...and things turned out just fine.

Don't let fear paralyze you—it's the ultimate inhibitor to your success. This doesn't mean you have to fly to Thailand and fight Muay Thai. It does, however, mean that fear is your biggest enemy. It robs you of growth, it suffocates you, and it's the reason so many people choose mediocrity. Complacency feels safe. It's not. It's a dream killer.

I don't care what your path is. Do not let your ambitions take a back seat to fear.

You get one shot at life. *One*. Take it for all it's worth, fear and all.

GROWTH THROUGH DISCOMFORT

Discomfort is the only pathway toward growth.

You grow stronger by going to the gym and pushing your body through pain. The best food for you tastes crappy. Saving money means giving up luxuries. That's how life works—the easy stuff doesn't make you better; the hard stuff does.

But believe me, the harder you work, the easier it will get. This is an American Dream 1.0 concept that will forever be an ingredient for success.

Write it down—what are some things you fear that are holding you back? Be honest with yourself. It may be completely unrelated to work. Is it a person? A thing? A situation?

We all have fears. That's normal. Choose to combat those fears and put yourself in uncomfortable situations. Test yourself. You have little to lose but a ton to gain. It starts with not turning a blind eye, and hitting it head-on!

CHAPTER 21

★ ★ ★

COMMANDING RESPECT VERSUS DEMANDING IT

What do you think of when you hear the letters *CEO*? Do you think of a tyrannical leader who barks orders at his employees? Do you think of greed and scandal? Sadly, those people do exist and are often magnified in the news media.

But greed and scandal are human flaws, not an economic class. There are plenty of broke greedy people, just as there are rich assholes. It's a character issue.

True leadership is hard to come by, and there is a big difference between leaders who command respect versus demand it. The latter is centered on ego and insecurities.

A true leader actually has a servant mindset.

A CEO by the name of Torrey Larsen is the epitome of a true servant leader.

Torrey Larsen is a friend and mentor of mine.

He is the CEO of Synergy One Lending, a national mortgage lender, now aligned with Mutual of Omaha Bank. A few years back, Synergy One was still a startup company. For a shot of growth in their company, they organized a mortgage conference for which I was the keynote speaker.

The conference was a huge success, and thousands of people attended.

As such, I was invited to the recap meeting back at Synergy One headquarters the following week. Torrey's entire team celebrated the great event. The primary purpose of the meeting was to figure out how to leverage the conference to continue the momentum.

But every time someone said something positive, this one

"wet blanket" in the room couldn't help but weigh the meeting down. For every opportunity for growth, he had an excuse for why they couldn't.

Torrey had seen enough. Torrey was one of the gentlest guys you could meet, but even the nice-guy CEOs have to show their teeth sometimes.

He stopped the meeting, stood up, and held his index fingers and thumbs in a pyramid.

He looked at the man we've now nicknamed "wet blanket."

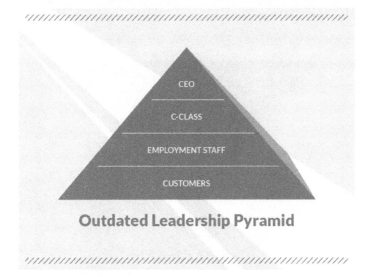

Outdated Leadership Pyramid

"What is this?" he asked.

"It's a triangle."

"That's right. This triangle is our company. You see my index fingers at the point up here? That's how you see everyone in this room. We're the executives and we sit at the top point of the triangle.

"In the middle are all of our employees, and here at my thumbs, at the widest part, are our customers. That's how you view things."

He then turned his finger triangle upside down so the widest part was at the top.

"This...this is how we are going to build our company."

True Leadership

He looked at the wet blanket and said, "As the CEO, I'm at the point here at the bottom. I'm only here to serve the needs of everyone above me. Everyone in this room and the rest of the C-suite is one notch above me, then our employees are just above that. The widest spot at the top is all of our customers. We serve from the bottom up, not the top down." Torrey paused for a moment. "Do you understand that?"

You could hear a pin drop.

It was the most authentic and wholesome ass-chewing of all time.

That wet blanket didn't last much longer at Synergy One, and the company itself exploded under Torrey's servant leadership. Eventually, they sold for an undisclosed number (let's just say it was a big one).

In the American Dream 2.0, being "the boss" and *demanding* respect, simply put, just isn't cool.

Servant leadership and commanding respect is a more well-received form of leadership. The rich guy at the top of the food chain shouting commands is not what people respond to anymore. There are way too many options, where nobody has to deal with this type of bullshit.

No amount of money can keep people in a company run by a tyrant.

Servant leaders put the needs of their employees and customers first, like Torrey Larsen.

As the CEO of a media company, I never use the term *employee*. We have a company culture built around being teammates. So that's what I call those who work *with* me, not *for* me.

You do not have to be the CEO of a company to take on this mindset.

- How can you be a servant leader?
- At your job?
- In your home?
- For your team?
- With your hobby?
- In your charity?
- Life is never a solo mission. How do you inspire others?

ACTION ITEMS

This mindset also exists in the world of creating content. As a thought leader, servant leadership applies to you. How do you serve your followers?

- Do you look up to them?

- Are you on the bottom of that triangle?

CHAPTER 22

★ ★ ★

"FAIL FORWARD"

The best mentors are willing to let you fail in order to learn a valuable lesson.

Or as my late mentor Ron used to say, "A setback is a setup for a comeback."

The first time I met Ron, he was fresh off a hip surgery. I only knew him from his speaking events, where he was a clean and polished speaker. I was lucky enough to get him on the phone to ask his advice about my business. It was 2008, and I was still in the mortgage game (during the massive market crash), leveraging our radio show as a primary marketing tool for our business.

I approached the phone call with Ron as formally as I could, starting with a simple "Hello. How are you?" I then asked as an icebreaker, "I saw on your recent webinar that you had hip surgery. How'd it go?"

He said, "My hip? You fucking kidding me? It sucks! I was running ten miles a day, and now I can't do shit."

That is how I was first introduced to Ron—*not* what I was expecting from the guy I've seen speaking on stages nationally!

Whoa!

I couldn't help but laugh out loud.

Here was this super-professional speaker I'd only seen on stage, and he was talking to me like a buddy at the bar. That was Ron, for better or for worse, and he was a little rough around the edges. Gotta appreciate authenticity.

"But let's get into it. Looks like your radio show is working well for you. How have you done it?"

"Well, we're a referral-based business, so we leverage the show to build those relationships."

"I don't understand," he said.

It was abundantly clear he wasn't impressed.

"We invite influencers and high-profile people in the community onto the show and ultimately build relationships with them. We build our content around them, bring them on the program, add a whole bunch of value to them, then we take them out to coffee, and yeah, they start referring us business. It's kinda cool, like a Trojan horse strategy. We give value first."

Ron's interest seemed to heighten. "So you now have referrals from some of the best referral sources in the market?"

"Exactly," I said.

Ron's response: "I have about thirty consulting clients who would piss themselves if you could teach them to do what you're doing." (I swear this is exactly what he said. Who talks like this?)

On our first phone call, we went from me asking for a consultation to us being in business together—immediately.

Within months, we had collaborated to create a product that taught other professionals how to do what I was doing in the way of media. It helped a ton of people improve their businesses. Like everything, we built it by adding value to our relationships.

A few months after Ron and I had developed that product, I was looking to make a move between companies in my own business.

He told me stories of his younger days as a consultant. He'd been an industry thought leader, and he'd been paid really well to align contractually with companies giving outside insight.

I was enthralled listening to his stories. Here I was, working in the trenches of the mortgage business—always working on commissions, working *late* hours seven days a week, never knowing for sure when my next payday would come—when I could be working as a paid consultant, not trapped in the trenches or subject to what at that time felt like hell: a market crash.

He shared with me, "When I was your age, I even got a few signing bonuses, too."

This was enough to convince me to jump ship.

Ron looked at me. I had no idea at the time, but he could see something I couldn't. He said, "Go ahead, Craig. Put together a proposal, send it to a few companies, and see what happens. *Go big.* You're worth it. Companies need you. You have the 'it factor.'"

That statement got to my head.

I managed to pique interest from some huge companies. They started flying me across the country for high-level meetings—that whole song and dance. If I could consult with them, it would be life-changing. One company told me to send a proposal with an offer.

With a slightly inflated ego that Ron had pumped up, I spent the next two weeks typing up a fifty-page manual highlighting my value as a consultant. Very American Dream 1.0 in the way I approached. Fifty pages, printed on expensive glossy paper, bound together at an office depot. Built it with my hands, not some online portal.

It was the first time I'd ever done something like this, and I didn't know my ass from a hole in the wall. I just knew that Ron said I was *The Man*, and I believed him!

On the last page of this beautifully bound document, I put my asking price. You don't need the details, but just know this: *I shot for the moon.*

I FedExed the proposal the day after I finished it, then met with Ron for lunch.

Meeting Ron for lunch usually meant a bottle of wine at a downtown San Diego restaurant. This time, it was in the heart of the Gaslamp District on a gorgeous San Diego day: 75 degrees and sunny.

I walked in with my head held high as Ron set down his

glass of wine, greeted me with a bro hug, and then poured me a glass.

"I sent the proposal out," I said.

"Good for you, Craig. I'm proud of you. Do you have a copy I could see?"

I slid an extra copy across the table toward him.

His body language was positive as he flipped through the proposal. I watched his grin grow, page after page. My confidence swelled as I tried to keep myself from smiling. After about fifteen minutes, he'd read the entire massive document.

Then he got to the last page and saw my asking price.

Suddenly, his body language changed. He squinted at the page and had to give it a few looks. You can imagine the quickly evaporating smile on my face.

He looked up at me and said with a chuckle, "Well, that's a bold offer," and started laughing!

"Um, yeah, man. You're damn right it's a bold offer. You told me to do that—you said I'm worth it."

"I told you to do *this?*"

I pointed at the proposal. "Yeah, *you* told me to do *this.*"

"*Me?* I told you to do *this?*"

Ron continued laughing and replied, "I must've been drunk when I said that."

He casually continued, "Don't worry, we'll soften this thing up a bit and then you can send it off."

"Ron, I just dropped it in the FedEx box this morning. It's already on its way!"

All of Southern California heard this man's roaring laugh.

So how did this fairy tale turn out? Not exactly the homerun I was looking for. The company didn't so much as pick up the phone to tell me to pound sand, let alone accept my offer. I never even heard back! Pretty funny in hindsight. It was a disappointment, but it's ultimately a valuable lesson learned.

To think I had just dropped that thing in a FedEx box, with the expectation they'd be calling me to ask where to send the big signing bonus. That was a weak way to state my worth. *Today*, too many people hide behind their computers, sending emails, rather than getting face-to-face.

Believe it or not, my biggest mistake wasn't my overpriced offer. That was fixable. The bigger lesson was that you shouldn't hide behind documents: man up/woman up and do your negotiations in person. What can be written or emailed is *never* as strong as standing up for yourself confidently in person.

In this story, if we had talked in person, they could make a counteroffer, and we could have had a discussion. Instead, they looked at the number on the last page of my proposal and likely tossed it like a Frisbee into their nearest trash can. Hell, they might've even taken it out back and set it on fire.

That's an old-school American Dream 1.0 strategy that we often forget about. We hide behind our keyboards instead of getting in the car or a plane and shaking people's hands face-to-face.

That failure taught me a very valuable lesson: when I was focused on providing value to other people, like with that product we'd developed, I was successful.

But once I focused on myself and how much money I thought I deserved because of ego, I failed, embarrassingly. Rather than say what you're worth, *be* what you're worth. Offers should be coming to me; I shouldn't have to draft anything. But truth be told, I was still wet behind the ears and had some learning to do.

Although Ron wouldn't call it a failure—it was a setback that set up a comeback—after I made the overpriced offer to that company, I met with another company *in person*.

To this day, we continue our partnership, and it's been a hell of a journey! We shook hands on a deal that included an equity stake and a more reasonable compensation model for both of us—one that was tied to *results*.

I'm no stranger to hard work and delivering on my value. I just need to be given the opportunity. Handshakes happen in person.

It was a win-win for both parties, and I never would have made that deal if it wasn't for the failure of the first one. When proposing your worth, there is no place for ego or overconfidence. Trade emails for handshakes, look someone in the eye, let them know your worth, and be willing to earn it.

ACTION ITEMS

No matter how good you get at something, you can never stop learning. There will always be someone who has achieved more than you. Find that person and learn from them, even if you never meet them in person. Webinars, for example, are a great way to constantly learn.

The concept of the mentor has changed drastically in the American Dream 2.0. Mentors can now even be online connections. Meeting mentors face-to-face is best, but that requires you to coordinate schedules with busy people. Sometimes you have to do that online. You can potentially learn anything you want from anyone you want anywhere in the world. There has never been a better time in history to learn from others. Mentoring can take on many forms; in the American Dream 2.0, you can find your teachers on YouTube. Even better, you can learn after hours.

CHAPTER 23

★ ★ ★

STEPHAN AARSTOL— USING FAILURE AS A SLINGSHOT TO SUCCESS

"The worst presentation in the history of *Shark Tank*."

Ouch! That can't be good for a brand right?

Stephan Aarstol, the owner of Tower Paddle Boards, shared his story on *The American Dream* with me—the story where he stood in front of five of the most iconic businesspeople in the world: Mark Cuban, Barbara Corcoran, Kevin O'Leary, Robert Herjavec, and Daymond John.

By the way, none of which impress me.

It's one thing to be "successful," but it's another thing to be an asshole who thinks money defines success. These guys *all* remind me of Simon Cowell from *American Idol* show ripping on young untalented singers to create a societal buzz. Dumb and mean. More reality TV crap.

Maybe one day Mark Cuban will babysit for Kanye West and Kim Kardashian on season 219 of *Keeping Up with the Kardashians*. I guess that could be interesting.

Until then, he's another blemish on modern-day media résumé and where things have gone terribly wrong in what society considers entertainment.

I imagine writing this in this book will cause him to fire up his attorneys to file a lawsuit on this book for my opinion of him. Napoleon complex causes guys like him to do things like this. I'm waiting.

Sorry, I digress.

That being said, Stephan was in the middle of the biggest presentation of his life, speaking on a national TV show.

And he forgot *everything*.

He was excited about his business, he loved his product, and he'd probably run through that exact moment in his head thousands of times before. But when he started the presentation, he sounded like he'd never spoken before.

Kevin O'Leary even said, "Don't worry, this is only the biggest moment of your life."

Rather than letting the momentary failure derail his entire presentation, Stephan pulled himself together and continued the pitch. He didn't let fear overcome him.

He overcame fear.

To my recollection—and I could be a little inaccurate on specifically how it went down from what Stephan shared with me—three of the sharks immediately dropped out, leaving just two: Mark Cuban and Kevin O'Leary.

Stephan started pitching his online marketing experience with previous startups. Cuban made him an offer. Stephan initially wanted $$$ in exchange for a small percentage of equity in Tower Paddle Boards. Instead, he gave up a big percentage of equity for $$$. It wasn't the deal he wanted, but you know what? He took the deal.

It was one of the best decisions of Stephan's business life.

When Cuban first invested on *Shark Tank*, Tower brought

in hundreds of thousands in revenue for the year. Just a few years later, their annual revenue was in the millions.

Stephan saw the walls caving in when he forgot his presentation. He turned what could have been an immediate failure into a deal and success story for his brand and business.

That's one of the biggest lessons you can learn in life: failure happens, but that doesn't mean you have to accept the failure. Now granted, I have no clue where the business stands today. But as Stephan shares with me, he turned lemons into lemonade. He had the wherewithal and confidence to turn his momentary failure into a long-term success.

We all face failures in business, presentations that flop, ideas that go south. We all face these failures. In life, too, not just business.

It doesn't matter whether you're living the American Dream 1.0 or 2.0. The mark of success isn't avoiding failure; it's moving forward *despite* failure.

Give yourself an honest assessment. What does a failure feel like to you? How do you respond to it? Do you find yourself like Stephan Aarstol: stop, regroup, and move forward, even if you risk embarrassment? While it might not be pretty, that type of resolve is confidence.

So, yes, they call it the worst presentation in the history of *Shark Tank*...that still got a deal.

Ultimately, Tower Paddle Boards has proven to be one of the most successful ventures in *Shark Tank* history, so I've heard.

CHAPTER 24

* * *

FAITH OVER FEAR

My worst mistake happened at age twenty—that age where we think we are invincible and know it all.

A knucklehead in college, when I got behind the wheel of a car after drinking. Granted, Uber didn't exist back then, but there is no excuse. I thank God every day that I didn't hurt someone and didn't learn a harder lesson than getting pulled over and going to jail.

The University of Missouri, where I was going to school at the time, had a new policy to suspend students with DUIs. So just before my final semester of school, I was suspended.

Suddenly, all of my friends were still in school, and I was a jobless ex-student with no money and no purpose. Life had just served me a big piece of humble pie, and I was left standing at a crossroad.

I remember the look on the advisory board as they kicked me out of the university. They seemed to take enjoyment out of it. But despite my anger toward them, this was my own doing.

I could either continue down this path of self-destruction and wind up a loser, broke, and in jail, or I could use my ambition for something other than partying.

I chose the path of change.

This was almost twenty years ago, before the days of online job searching. I had to pull out a newspaper and do it American Dream 1.0 style—by looking at the job ads in the classifieds.

I found a part-time job as a telemarketer for a mortgage company. Even telemarketing doesn't exist anymore. I quickly moved up to a position as an assistant loan officer. Actually, that happened in the very first day. I put all of my ambition into that job and moved up quickly.

Before long, I was nobody's assistant but rather my own mortgage professional, and soon thereafter managing the branch.

At twenty-one years old, I got a quick taste at a young age of what six figures felt like. All the while, I was still living with my two college roommates, paying $200 a month rent. They were still in college party mode. While they were up partying till sun-up, I was putting on a tie and going to work.

Life had punched me in the nose, but I got up swinging. When my suspension was up, I went back to school, doubling up as a full-time student and a full-time business professional. I would skip all my classes for work and just cram for the tests—not exactly a sustainable model.

It all came to a head. I had to study for a final exam, but like always, I delayed until the last minute. I remember the moment clear as day: I was sitting in a Cracker Barrel, a fine Missouri establishment (sense sarcasm here).

I went to open the course textbook for the first time all semester and noticed my vision was blurry. I looked up, and everything sounded like I was in an echo chamber.

Call it anxiety, call it a panic attack, call it anything you want. Whatever it was, it was weird, and it was a turning point. I shut the book and said to myself, "I'm done."

I quit college at a Cracker Barrel.

That was it.

I walked away from the University of Missouri and never looked back.

It was my fault I chose to get behind a wheel.

I deserved all the trouble I put myself in. An embarrassment I'll never live down and one that I reluctantly share in this book. But it's part of my story. And quite honestly, it provided me the most valuable lesson I strongly needed at that time in my life.

But I'll never forget that moment sitting in front of ten older men and women from the university, all looking at me like I was some hopeless kid with no future. With a tape recorder capturing everything from the middle of the table, they told me I was done. I walked into the hallway with tears in my eyes.

One of the men followed me out. "Hey, Craig, hold on a second."

I thought he was about to offer me a saving grace and say that they'd changed their mind.

"You forgot this." He handed me my notepad.

Some saving grace.

At twenty years old, I needed to make some life changes, and now I had the motivation to do so. Crazy to think that that was the last time I ever drank and drove...and the best thing that ever happened to me. And it was also the last time I'd be known as just some hopeless kid with no future.

I had something to prove. While my friends partied, I made dramatic changes. That's what failures and mistakes are: an opportunity to pull together and reassess your life.

It's these moments you look back on when you get older. It was one of the worst moments of my life. Hell, the way I was behaving, I *was* hopeless.

What ended up being a very dark hour of my life ended up being one of the greatest lessons. Failures are not catastrophic events; they are simply opportunities to learn.

Think back to moments that you've failed.

- What lessons did you learn?
- What lessons can you still learn?
- Are those lessons valuable to you today?
- What did they teach you?
- How did they make you a better person?

Now look forward.

When you can replace the fear of failure with faith that in the very worst moments you are still learning valuable lessons, *you become unstoppable.*

GROWTH THROUGH SACRIFICE

Everybody wants to have it all—the leisure and the success. That's not the way it worked in the American Dream 1.0 or the American Dream 2.0 either.

We have the privilege of working hard for our dreams. Most other countries do not give you this opportunity.

The most successful people in this country work hard. That's the one thing you can control: how hard you are willing to work. And truth is, so many people just aren't willing to. The grind is too uncomfortable.

There are no shortcuts to success, and that means you have to make sacrifices.

Success might require you to give up the vices, such as watching TV, partying, or even your friends (sometimes, you simply outgrow people). It's up to you to determine what's important.

Once you start cutting out the bullshit, it'll become obvious real quickly who has your best interests at heart and who wants to hold you down with the rest of them.

Sometimes growth means letting go of old habits and old friendships. That's sacrifice, and it's not easy. But sacrifice of one kind or another is necessary to be successful.

CHAPTER 25

* * *

PERFECTLY IMPERFECT

I stood offstage, nervously flipping through my note cards as I muttered the words to myself. I had the speech memorized down to the *pauses* between words. I might as well have been a robot reading lines from a script.

It was 2006, and I was putting on my first big professional event. Public speaking still terrified me, so I'd spent weeks writing and memorizing my lines. Somehow, I got through my speech. Honestly, I blacked out for most of it, so I just assumed it came across okay.

After the event, one of the headlining speakers, a true professional named Steve Harney—a *big* New York guy both in size and personality, with a thick Brooklyn accent—needed a ride to the airport. Steve heads a blog called "Keeping Current Matters" and is an overall awesome guy.

"How did I do with my speech, Steve?"

He said, "Craig, you're a great guy with a big heart. Being imperfect and authentic is a much stronger skillset than memorizing your lines."

It hurt, as honest feedback often does, but he was right. Steve was the man, and like a typical New Yorker, he did me a service in just shooting it to me straight when he could've easily gone the other way. Tough love, they call it.

It's funny how life works out, since I'm now a national TV show host and a public speaker. I am often in the position of coaching other speakers. My key ingredient in mentoring others is by practicing radical authenticity.

As Gary Vaynerchuk once put it, "People's bullshit meter is at an all-time high," especially millennials.

With so much garbage and phoniness online, people are intrigued by what's *real*. And by real, I don't mean like reality TV, which is as fake as it gets. I'm talking *real*, raw, and relatable.

The only way to do that is by being radically authentic. Also, like my last chapter illustrates, being vulnerable. Social media has a funny way of tricking society into depression thinking everyone else is perfect.

So if we try and pretend we are something we're not, it's obvious.

Nobody is a perfect speaker. I'd rather see someone imperfect and unscripted than perfectly scripted. Manufactured content reeks of disingenuousness. Get out of your head and get in your heart.

Those who don't like you for who you truly are aren't worth an ounce of your concern.

ROBERTO MONACO

If you ever think you have an excuse for not reaching your American dream, remember the story of Roberto Monaco, a frequent guest on our show (@theamerican-dreamtv, and @craigsewingmedia for some Roberto quotes and clips).

Roberto came to America from Brazil in his early thirties knowing zero English.

Roberto sought out Tony Robbins at an event and demanded a job as a salesperson despite the language difficulties. He taught himself English and became a top salesperson for Robbins. He then went on to become the CEO of Influenceology, a company that coaches people on public speaking.

Think about that…Roberto now teaches persuasion and speaking skills in a country where *he didn't even know the language when he moved here*. Now *that* is the American dream!

If you think you're not a good enough speaker or don't like yourself on camera, or your content isn't good enough for your business, just think about Roberto Monaco.

He didn't have some special speaking skill that everyone else lacked. He simply let his ambition guide him, and that was enough.

CHAPTER 26

* * *

BALANCE IS BULLSHIT

Balance is bullshit. As far as I'm concerned, find what you love and move forward full speed ahead.

Love does not have limitations. You can love many aspects of your life, with 100 percent of your heart to give toward it. Your spouse, kids, hobbies, career, etc. While all of them are different, no reason to not be fully in love with *all* of them. One does not have to take from the other.

Balance is something preached so often by those who've already made it. It's what unhappy people say to reduce distaste they have for the work area of their life. Granted, there are times to turn your phone off, such as while you're on a date. That's a little different.

What I'm referring to is this idea that you should need some sort of counterbalance to how hard you work. If you love what you do, then it solves for itself. In fact, if you love what you do, it's not work.

Point is, you can love everything important to you unconditionally—just in different ways. It kills me when people advise others to "work hard, then take a vacation." My advice is to love your work so much that it's as cool as a vacation...and yeah, go on trips, too. I am not an "or" person; I am an "and" person. Do both!

Taking a vacation to balance work stress is like riding a bike. If you just sit there, you'll tip over. How do you balance? KEEP MOVING FORWARD.

Overcompensation is not balance. Love your family with every ounce of passion during family time. Love your work with every ounce of passion when it's work time. Love your hobbies *after* you have those first two in order. In that way, all those worlds can coexist. And more.

And there is *plenty* of time for all of it, too. Just make sure that when you are giving someone or something your time, you give them or it your full attention.

If you love what you do, you'll find natural balance. If you are not excited to get out of bed every morning for everything, that to me is a lack of balance. The solution is, change your line of work. But here's the big point.

With the American Dream 2.0, the game has changed! It doesn't have to be about college, then college debt, trying forever to pay it off while working the corporate ladder stuck in your 9:00–5:00 p.m. The entrepreneurial spirit is alive more than ever. It doesn't mean everyone's cut out for it, but the opportunity exists. We are all CEOs of *ourselves*!

Now, I've referenced the ability to learn things on You-Tube, to leverage social media platforms for marketing, and all the new age digital strategies that were not there in the American Dream 1.0.

But there is even more to it.

Even if you *do* have a job, just the ability to work remotely is incredible. It wasn't that long ago that you had to be in an office to check your email. And before that, your *mail*. Now, that device in your hand can put you on an island in the Caribbean and yet still stay connected to the real world.

You know what smartphones and apps do more than anything? They make things easier. That's their whole point. There are so many apps that can do things for you—

virtual assistants, CRMs, budgeting, etc. You can have a full workforce in the palm of your hand. *Recognize* the brilliance.

Will you have to learn some new things?

Yes.

Old dogs that don't want to learn the new tricks will die off in the American Dream 1.0. The apps now even make the non-tech-savvy people tech savvy. You have *the choice* to do what you love, the resources to be educated to do it well, and the tools to build around it—right there at your fingertips.

This is where that old-school American Dream 1.0 can really lose its admirability and just be called plain dumb. There's the expression "Can't teach old dogs new tricks." I didn't make that shit up. That saying exists for a reason. It means something.

Don't let it be referring to you!

Don't get me wrong, some people are perfectly happy in their nine-to-five job. If that's you, great—no judgment here. This message is for those people who aren't happy, who complain but do nothing about it. Life is too short and too full of opportunity to complain about anything but especially your job.

In the American Dream 2.0, there are more opportunities now than in the history of humankind to chase your dream. What's keeping you from doing it?

Is it fear? Fear can be a paralyzer. Turn fear into faith. Remember, even in failure you learn and grow. The only thing holding you back is *you*!

Sometimes it's easy to procrastinate. Sometimes we get caught in paralysis by analysis. But now is not just a good time; it's *the* time. Remember, the number one—as in you get only *one* life.

What's holding you back from doing what you love?

ACTION ITEMS

I want you to get out a pen and paper and list some things out.

- What do you *love*?

- What are you good at?

- What are your gifts?

- If you could do this every day of your life, what would it look like?

Next list:

- What's holding you back?

- Specifically, why?

Next list:

- What skills do you *think* you need?

- What tools do you *think* you need?

- What resources do you *think* you need?

ACTION: Now, as simple as this is, Google your solution.

I am always shocked when I realize that when I'm trying to figure something out, all I had to do was type it into YouTube, and there are video solutions.

Virtual assistant? Google it.

Better time management? Google it.

How to raise money for an idea? Google it.

Damn near everything exists in today's online marketplace.

CHAPTER 27

* * *

WHO DO YOU SERVE?

The world is begging for innovators.

A few years after that conference, where Bob Pittman told everyone in radio that they were dinosaurs, the station my show was on, KCBQ 1170 AM, was trying to stay relevant by putting on events, like live radio shows with audiences and nationally syndicated hosts.

I had some experience now, and I was making a decent living from radio. But let's face it, this still wasn't my space.

This event was at the Hall of Champions in San Diego, which was a prestigious venue, with cool sports memorabilia and theater staging. I stood in the back of the auditorium watching the nationally recognized hosts do their live shows.

The GM of our station, we'll call him Dave, made his way toward me and watched by my side. He was a super-nice, old-school American Dream 1.0 kind of guy. He was heavyset, soft-spoken, and had his shirt tucked into his jeans. He looked like he'd been in radio for forty years because, well actually, he had.

Dave came of age in the '70s and '80s, when radio was all sex, drugs, and rock and roll. I gotta imagine it was their heyday financially, too. But now YouTube, Facebook, podcasts, and the future had come in to break up the monopoly. The country had also recently experienced a market crash, so the whole world was upside down.

Here I was, standing next to him at this event for our station, as people around the country were getting laid off, and shows were getting canceled, and I was clueless with no concept of radio's glory days. Here's a dose of reality. Why on earth would they have even offered me a radio show in the first place? That in itself proved the market had turned, and they were desperate for money. What the hell did I know about hosting a show? Not much. They didn't care.

Dave shook his head. "You know, Craig, it's been a

tough run in this space." He looked around at the crowd watching the live event, and you could see in his eyes that he knew the good ol' days were nothing but a distant memory. He spoke of the "dying industry."

I said, "Dave, man, I love radio. I don't know, maybe I'm just naive and don't know how it's supposed to work, but our show is crushing it. I've been having a lot of fun with it."

He looked at me, put his hand on my shoulder, and said something I will never forget: "Craig, the fact that you're so naive is one of your greatest strengths. Others get bogged down by how it used to be, whereas you just decide to make it how it is."

He didn't have to explain any further.

I knew exactly what he meant.

He meant the reason so many of his friends, coworkers, and colleagues across the nation were losing their ass was because they were those old dogs who were refusing to learn new tricks. They turned their nose up at podcasts and called social media a fad.

They clung to old data and taught sales strategies selling *against* the new mediums.

But as a naive as I was, I didn't have that anchor attached to my leg, I didn't romanticize about the past, and that allowed me to venture forth fearlessly into the unknown. I was the most uneducated in most rooms, and that was my biggest strength.

Think about it for a second.

As you ponder what the future might look like, the natural onset of fear and procrastination might set in.

Do not be scared of what's unknown; instead, be motivated by it. The one thing I have learned—often the toughest thing to do—is to just make the decision. Start putting one foot in front of the other. Go.

Once you make the big decisions in life, it's one of the best ways to throw that bridge into the canyon. As Tony Robbins puts it, "You can't take the island unless you burn the boats." That commitment will be the key ingredient to your success.

Do you honestly think once you set your mind to something, you'll want to prove yourself wrong? Pride alone will be a source of your success. Think about that one for a minute.

If you make that big decision, the fuel to your fire is to prove yourself right. That's all the motivation you need.

Don't let fear paralyze you.

And just like how my career in media started with radio, something I knew nothing about, the unknown is not as scary as you think.

YOU WILL BE OBSOLETE EVENTUALLY—WHO CARES?

There will come a point when (almost) everything I write in this book will be obsolete. I'm okay with that. One day, I'll be writing *The American Dream 3.0*.

To a certain extent, most things you do will be obsolete in a few years, too. The one guarantee with change is that it's constant. The world keeps turning, and so should you. Never stop moving forward.

If you're young, old, grew up chasing the American Dream 1.0 or 2.0, it doesn't matter. As long as you're willing to adapt to the fast-paced world we live in, nobody has an advantage on you.

If you're willing to work hard, build relationships, and invest in yourself, you have every shot at your American dream.

CHAPTER 28

* * *

PUKE IT OR LOSE IT

"Okay, fellas, two minutes to showtime."

Our producer walked out the door, leaving just me and my business partner waiting to begin our first show. As the countdown began, he stood up and rushed out of the studio.

Where the hell is he going? He's supposed to open the show!

The countdown dropped to thirty seconds and he still wasn't back. Twenty seconds...still nothing. Then, just as our intro music, AC/DC's "Money Talks," blasted through the studio, he finally rushed back in and took his seat. He looked like he'd seen a ghost, and his white T-shirt was soaking wet.

Without acknowledging me, he muttered his way through

a live show open. And then without any warning whatso-ever, he totally bailed on his piece and *dumped it on me*: "And Craig, what do you think?"

Um...huh? Here I was, staring at the studio microphone completely unprepared to talk.

That's not how we rehearsed this thing. He was supposed to open the show; I was supposed to come in later.

But I was handed a proverbial "shit or get off the pot" moment, so I had no choice but to ramble some nonsense into a mic for God knows how long. The time it took to get to our first commercial break felt like an eternity. I'm pretty sure I blacked out through the whole thing, just like when I gave my first speech.

After we finished, I asked him what had happened.

"I was so nervous I had to go puke in the bathroom."

I laughed so hard I just about got sick myself. We've laughed about that moment for years. How pathetic we must have sounded to people driving in their cars lis-tening to our show. Good news is, at that time, nobody was really listening anyway. If only they could have seen two grown-ass men behaving like little children scared of some boogeyman. What the hell were we scared of?

As I now have a TV show and coach in media, I often find people terrified of seeing themselves on video. Why? If anything, it means you're narcissistic. Stop obsessing over yourself in ways that nobody else does about you.

But as time went on, we got better. The next thing we knew, the nerves faded away, and we didn't even puke before shows anymore. That was a champagne moment. Then, outta nowhere, people started calling in.

People actually started listening to us. We invited influencers from the business community onto the show. We took pictures with them, went to coffee after the shows, and built relationships with people...American Dream 1.0 style.

Our show was a Trojan horse strategy to relationships that we ultimately leveraged outside of the show. The next thing we knew, our radio show was more successful than our actual back-end business we started it for.

Taking risks is almost always worth it—even if they make you puke.

Now this all makes for a fun story, but seriously, what thing do you fear the most that you know is good for you? I know I keep beating this dead horse, but I see it every day. People who have the greatest opportunity *ever* to live their dreams don't—because of fear or just living a habitual life. If there is anything you get from this book, I want it to be motivation to chase your dreams.

Let's talk about how this can relate to marketing of your brand.

I always say, "You can't gain market *share* without being a great market*er*."

In the American Dream 1.0, the Salad Bowl had customers in its neighborhood because it had a great story. People talked about it, and because of that, the line was always long in that little cafeteria. It was known in the neighborhood.

It had a great story.

Today, you have a significantly bigger megaphone for connectivity and storytelling at your disposal in the form of *content*, video, digital marketing, and social media. It still all needs to lead back to *real* relationships. Trade those emails for handshakes, but cast that wide net.

What keeps you from creating content related to your passion projects?

Nerves?

Get out of your head and get into your heart. You got something to say? Then say it.

Stop worrying about the judgment of others. Hate to break it to you, but nobody cares how your hair looks or if your message has imperfections. They care about your message and you. And if they don't, then that's not your ideal customer anyway. There are *plenty* more out there.

What's your story?

That little phone in your hand has a camera that is more powerful than some of the most advanced cameras in history. You can create a video and post it online right now with a few clicks.

Gary Vaynerchuk started Wine Library, a $60-million business on a Flip cam and YouTube, and he'd be the first to tell you, it was terrible. But you know what? He was *consistent*.

And it costs you *nothing*.

In the American Dream 2.0, your story matters now, more than ever. Whether people look you up, Google you, and you are defining what they find, or you are projecting content out to the masses, what is your story? What do you stand for? Some might call it your brand, your niche, etc.

I call it your story.

CHAPTER 29

* * *

ICE CREAM FOR BREAKFAST

Bad food makes you feel bad, and good food makes you feel healthy.

Pretty simple.

If you ate ice cream every day for breakfast, lunch, and dinner, how do you think you'd feel? The same goes for the information you consume, except what makes this trickier is it's affecting an organ that's much more complex and you can't see it. If you eat like crap, you're going to not only feel it, but you're also going to *see* it.

If you consume negative information, it's not as easy to quantify what you are feeding your subconscious. In a world with a 24/7 news cycle, predicated on ratings, the stuff we are being fed is *crap*. Sadly, it works, because the sheeple will click on the links that lead to the story that drives the advertising dollars.

National news? Crap.

Local news? Crap. We've seen enough car wrecks and robberies.

Pop culture? Crap. The Kardashians are the worst creation in the history of humankind.

You get the point.

As for *The American Dream Show*, within our media model, has always been about combatting negative media. It's our mantra. Whether it be those who view our content or our partners who support it, having a unified purpose has been proven to accelerate our growth.

People are sick and tired of being sick and tired. Regardless of if you own a media company, *everything* is media related. Your brand lives online. Your personality lives online.

That's media.

I *do believe* society as a whole and the infatuation with

social media is a growing problem. Personally, if it wasn't the place commerce happened, I could care less about it.

Our journey started in radio, evolving to TV, created the launch of our media company, and it is now very robust and diverse among all mediums. All of which is held together by real relationships.

Now we have a national TV show called *The American Dream* where millions are influenced through our content. In the American Dream 1.0, our journey would not have been possible. Only in the American Dream 2.0 could we not be owned by a network, be commercial-free, and have no advertisers—only partners. We were truly self-made trailblazers in a world where you can throw all the way things "used to be" out the window. A perfect environment for a serial entrepreneur like myself. A perfect environment for *you*, no matter what your ambition.

We were successful enough; we found ourselves in an event in Southern California, surrounded by major cable stations and affiliated networks: the Emmy Awards.

That's right.

This clueless guy from Missouri, with no understanding of media, was invited with his production team to an Emmy nomination party.

No idea what it meant, but it sounds cool, right?

There we were, this little independent entrepreneurial media company with no affiliation to the networks. Again, we were outsiders. We didn't fit in.

And it became very easy to see why.

We were invited to an event to see if we would be nominated for an Emmy that eventually led to the big stage...I think.

Honestly, I don't even care how it works; it's all politics. I'm too busy building something real, rather than play the phony game. The nominations started happening. A mile-long list of potential nominations and nominees, surrounded by those wetting their pants to be there.

Here's how those awards started to be announced:

Best earthquake coverage goes to...

Best coverage of the California fires goes to...

Best coverage of the Las Vegas shooting goes to...

It was a mile-long list of topics like this.

The last one pissed me off.

As the nominees were announced, those who heard their names called jumped up, hugged, high-fived, celebrated, whatever.

My team and I just sort of stared at ourselves, as if we were in the twilight zone.

The guy on stage just announced, "Best coverage of the Las Vegas shooting," and you're jumping for joy?

It was so surreal to us, that this was something to celebrate.

Our entire model of the American dream was centered on positivity and inspiration.

In regard to the Vegas shooting, they announced all of the nominees without so much as a mention of the heroes from that day or, God forbid, honoring those who lost their lives in the tragedies.

Could we at least do that first?

Before simply high-fiving some bimbo on camera for how she covered it or the videography team trapped in the cable network zoo like a lion in a cage? There is no honor in that! How does that make the world a better place?

How many people in that room could honestly say that they'd focused on the positives from that tragic day rather than the killer? It seems the media *loves* to plaster the psychopath's name and face everywhere but ignores those who died and those who even saved lives—the true heroes.

What do those priorities say about our values as a country?

I'd seen glimpses of it before, but in that moment, I saw the real face of America's major media outlets. And it was vomit worthy. They rewarded each other for highlighting mass killers rather than breathing oxygen into the positive stories.

Like Taylor Winston.

You probably don't know him nor would you. He got very little recognition after the Vegas shooting. Taylor is a man we interviewed on *The American Dream* within a week after the tragedy.

Why?

Taylor is the marine who, instead of running from the scene of the Las Vegas shooting, found a pickup truck, stole it, and loaded it hauling the victims off to the hospital. Trip after trip, he put his life at risk and saved lives.

He was a hero among the horror. And you know what? There were many others who did similar acts of courage.

How much did you hear about him versus how much did you hear about the killer?

Isn't this how all the mass shootings have played out?

They chose to highlight the killer instead of Taylor Winston. They ensured that the next psychopath with a gun will do the same thing. It's predictable at this point with these network clowns and what they call news or stories.

Here's the secret, though: *they want us in fear.*

That's how they make their money. I read an op-ed piece from a higher-up at CNN admitting it. They measure our views and clicks, sell it to advertisers, create ratings...Cha-ching. Reality TV. Do you really think this became popular because it's *real*? Nowhere near. I've been on these shows before; there is nothing real about them whatsoever.

I mean, look: of course you have to report some negative things on the news—that's the world we live in—but they *obsess* over it. Do we really need a 24/7 news cycle? That's why cable news doesn't have a place in the American Dream 2.0: it's not real journalism anymore. Journalism is dead.

The news is now full of garbage you'd find in the checkout line of the grocery store. It doesn't help you feel better, and it doesn't help you grow professionally, personally, spiritually, or financially. So what's the point?

Be careful what you put into your mind: garbage in, garbage out. It's the equivalent of eating ice cream every day for your meals.

In the American Dream 2.0, there is an abundant way to access healthier information to grow. Inspiring content is in abundance.

Treat what you consume mentally similarly to what you consume orally. Is it healthy? Is it good for me? Does this make me a better person? That negative news embeds into your subconscious, and it's just a waste of time. Some of this might sound basic, but then again, it's important!

If you want to accomplish your American Dream 2.0, you need to be efficient with your time. Time is your most valuable asset. Twenty-four hours in a day is *a lot*. You can learn an insane amount of new skills each and every day by simply dedicating to things that matter, not to mention the mental state.

Consume negative content—what's that going to do?

Does it make you happier or more cynical? Friendly or more argumentative?

As for that Emmy nomination party, after the Vegas shooting nominations, my team had enough. My producer Dylan looked up at me and said, "Let's get the hell out of here."

We left our seats and took everyone next door to a dive bar where we took tequila shots and said cheers, proud to be outcasts.

Do I still have the ambition to win an Emmy?

I do.

But it will be on our terms, for content that matters. In the meantime, we are an entrepreneurial model; awards are for the birds. We're about making an impact. And so should you be.

CHAPTER 30

* * *

"MOOD ROULETTE"

That's what news has become, but let's talk a little about other content consumption.

Content is king. Distribution is queen but wears the pants.

Let's share with you a story about a guy named Rich. He was a partner of ours for *The American Dream*. One day he said to me, "Craig, man, I love partnering with you and your company. But when you talk about things we should be doing on social media, I gotta be honest. Man, I *hate* social media!"

I replied, "Yeah, man, me, too."

He was taken aback by my response.

"Huh?"

"Yeah, I think it's nauseating. And as far as business, a bunch of people hiding behind their computers, not building real relationships."

Rich replied, "But you're the CEO of a media company, and you say how important it is."

Well...Yeah, it is. But if it wasn't important, I could care less. You think I need to waste my time scrolling through people's opinions, life coaching, or narcissistic selfies? I don't.

But there's more to it.

And let me be clear as we live in this American Dream 2.0 digital world. Social media is *one* spoke on the wheel. Technology, digital marketing, email campaigning, leveraging apps, and simply being able to be on an island in the Bahamas while running a business—*that* is what makes the American Dream 2.0 incredible. The game has expanded.

I said, "Rich, what don't you like about social media?"

"People on it are annoying and nauseating."

Okay.

Well, I gave Rich two pieces of advice: "You realize you

can *unfollow* annoying and nauseating people, right? You realize that you yourself don't have to be annoying and nauseating on there, right?"

Problem solved.

It's really a choice on what you consume, and it's a choice of what you put out there.

As a society, we are addicted to the nonsense, regardless of the medium it's found on. Not because we want to be, but because it's been forced down our throats. It starts with being conscious of what you consume.

It really is a choice.

Choose what you consume and when you consume it.

Here's a simple example. I *refuse* to start my day in bed with my phone in my hand. No phones in bed. It's like playing "mood roulette." When you start your day by reading your emails or checking Facebook, you are allowing the first thing you experience that day to be what randomly shows up on that screen. A negative email or an ugly storyline can derail your entire day. I also think there is something terribly wrong with our obsession with technology and forgetting the tangible things in life.

Ditch it.

I start every day without an alarm clock. I don't need one. I've designed my life that way.

It doesn't mean I don't get up early to get after it; I just don't let some device "alarm me" and tell me to get up (there are exceptions to this obviously). Before I even get out of bed, I take some deep breaths and think about what I'm grateful for. I also think, *What would a successful day look like today?* Every single day gives us this incredible reset button. There aren't too many things I love more than watching the sunrise, giving me the opportunity to leave things behind yesterday and start anew today.

I always start my day getting fresh air, taking deep breaths, stretching a bit.

And thinking about everything I am grateful for, big and small alike.

Appreciating the roof over my head, a fridge with food in it, and hearing a bird chirp remind me that I'm alive. I set the tone for my day, not my electronic, or worse, someone else's random opinion that showed up in front of me for scrolling through it.

The whole world is going to be overwhelming for the day, but my time in the morning is my time with me.

ACTION ITEMS

Are you cognizant of the content you consume?

Is it positive or negative?

Does it do you any good?

Do you take control at the start of the day, or do you play "smartphone roulette" and leave it up to someone else?

You have access to almost any information you could ever want online. It can be a blessing or a curse, depending on how you use it. You're the CEO of *you*; be your own boss. Win every day. It starts with mindset.

CHAPTER 31

★ ★ ★

MINDSET

There is no better time than the present. Life has become one big sensory overload.

Let's be honest, in the American Dream 1.0, things were a little more humanized and real.

You wake up, and your phone blinks at you with a new notification. The talking head on TV tells you about the latest tragedy in your state. You read an email from someone hiding behind their own computer, and they toss you something negative that messes up your whole day or, in the very least, shifts your energy just a bit.

You spend your day typing away on a computer or poking away on a smartphone. How are you supposed to navigate this world without losing your damn mind?

It's truly a sensory overload. No wonder everybody's been diagnosed with ADD and anxiety. You think it's a coincidence the country is more hooked on prescription drugs than ever before? You think it's odd that people are losing their shit and shooting people? It's a serious societal crisis we face.

We're not going to solve world problems with this book, but I do hope to provide some guidance that empowers your mentality.

The beauty of life is that you get to live it. Every day gives you a new opportunity for an appreciation of that very fact, a reset of anything that held you back yesterday, and the opportunity to today to make progress.

PERSPECTIVE IS EVERYTHING

One hundred and fifty thousand people die every day. But you're alive. Be thankful for that, if nothing else. The odds that you're even alive are a slim-to-none miracle. There's no law in the universe that says you had to be born. I promise you, the struggles you face and what we fall into the habit of calling "stress" ain't that bad.

But we can go a layer deeper. In the times of American Dream 1.0, mental strength was critical to success. Long hours, hard work, the grind...Quite honestly, our grandparents *should* turn over in their graves embarrassed by the societal mental weakness. It's gotten to be pretty pathetic. We give tenth-place trophies now!

I'll never forget the time a company I was involved with had an employee who quit. I was called into a meeting of six higher-ups, where they wanted me involved. They went around the room on how to properly let this person go, reports that needed to be filed, things that needed to be documented, and on and on in fear of getting sued. I was mind-boggled.

You do realize, she quit, right? You're not even firing her!

But in the American Dream 2.0, we have to be honest with ourselves. Life moves *fast*.

That speed can play tricks on you, creating stress and anxieties that are different than the days when you had significantly less stimulation.

Earlier I said, "Balance is bullshit." I meant that in reference to this belief that you should find ways to compensate for your work by things like vacation. You should love your work *and* vacation. Truth is, balance is not a compensation model but rather an expectation model. Being content where you are is a beautiful thing. The single biggest discovery in my personal *and* professional career (which pretty much could be called life) is meditation—something that is hard to believe with hard-charged guys like me.

I recall a conversation with a friend once where I exclaimed meditation's importance to me. He replied, "You meditate? Yeah, right. You're the last person I'd expect to meditate."

You might be thinking the same thing just reading this book.

Let me tell you, that's *exactly* why I need it more than most.

Depression comes from getting hung up on things in your past and anxieties from worrying about the future. All this comes from the subconscious mind, which is designed to protect you. It's the part of your mind that makes your heart beat at this very moment. You're not having to remember to do that, or 99 percent of your life, or even remembering to breathe. The brain puts you on autopilot. It does that a lot, and this is why training your brain is critical. There is always a book on my nightstand about this subject matter.

To solve for almost every moment of mental friction is to be present. Calm that subconscious chatter.

If there is any piece of advice I want you to take to heart, it's the importance of mindfulness. Granted, a lot of people are talking about this these days. Good! There are snake oil salesmen in this space as well. Use your best judgment and ignore them.

I am going to repeat this.

Meditation is the single most important discovery of my life. I have nothing to "sell you" with that statement. You've already bought the book. My genuine care for you is your success, and nothing is more important than your state of mind. Life is crazy; I know you are "too busy." But you absolutely must carve out time in your day for you—and only you.

A dear friend of mine said to me once, "With me working so much and the kids, I feel guilty not spending all free time I have with them."

Excuse.

You'll make a better dad if you can give your kids a better version of you. Find fifteen minutes for yourself.

This book will not dive deep into meditation, but I am incredibly passionate about it.

That is why I am hammering you hard on its importance.

Buy books on it. It's the American Dream 2.0. Just Google or YouTube it. But take it seriously.

I believe it could solve many of the metaphorical illnesses our country has. Eliminate the need for drugs or any fix to distract us from the mental conflict we endure on a day-to-day basis. I believe it should be taught to kids in school, it should be a normality for adults, and in the very least, it should be something you take to heart from this book.

The argument of "I don't have time to do this every day" tends to be made. My thought: If you don't have fifteen minutes a day for yourself, find an hour. I promise you, you'll love the results. And as far as I'm concerned, your success in an American Dream 2.0, fast-paced world requires it.

THE MYTH OF THE QUICK FIX

The quick fix doesn't exist. Yet our lives are dominated by things designed to save time.

What is the smartphone but a device that makes things faster? Remember when we used to sit at a desktop computer and wait for AOL to connect to the internet for thirty, even sixty seconds? That weird sound it used to make when connecting?

Now we freak out when our Uber is more than a block away or if our Facebook doesn't load fast enough.

Technology has advanced so quickly that we forgot how slow everything was just a few years ago in the American Dream 1.0. There is something really good about the "good ol' days."

We're so focused on getting from A to Z that we skip the twenty-four letters in between. A lot of those steps between where we are and where we want to be are imperfections, which can be beautiful.

Even if a quick fix did exist (which it doesn't), you'd never want it, because you'd miss out on the unexpected and imperfect beauty of life. Enjoy the journey more than your rush for some end result. Sometimes in an American Dream 2.0 world, that takes reminding ourselves frequently and setting aside time to practice it.

Truth is, no matter how difficult your life gets, it could be a lot worse. You didn't have to be born and you don't have to be alive, but you won the lottery of life by being born in the United States.

CHAPTER 32

★ ★ ★

THAT "OH SHIT" MOMENT

The Navy SEAL team that took out Osama bin Laden will forever be remembered as heroes. A book written about it called *No Easy Day* highlights their accomplishment. But nobody talks about the preparation that went into that mission. It was far more than just one day's work.

Based off satellite imagery, the navy created a replica of bin Laden's compound on a base in the United States. For months, SEAL Team Six trained in the exact conditions they'd experience during the real mission. Actually, it was a replicated version of it. There is no way to create exact conditions of an event like invading a compound in the middle of the night in Pakistan.

In preparation, they'd fly their helicopters into the real

compound and either capture bin Laden alive or take him out. This was the plan. But their mission didn't go according to plan. What makes the SEALs, well, the SEALs is part of their planning: they plan for unforeseen events— that "oh shit" moment where things don't go as expected.

The teams took off in the middle of the night, flying in two helicopters toward bin Laden's compound in Pakistan. As they approached, one of their choppers wrecked, almost killing the SEAL team. In the chaos, they improvised based on their training. They didn't let the panic consume them. Instead, they worked together as a team and created an alternate route to accomplish their mission.

As I share this story, please pause for a moment. Think about this: these guys were flying in the middle of the night to break into a terrorist compound, unknowing of what they would find, and *everything* went to shit as one of the helicopters crashed. Can you imagine this? Mind-blowing!

They continued into the heart of the compound, took out bin Laden in a firefight in his home, and still had the presence of mind to take all the files, computers, and hard drives they could carry back into the one remaining chopper.

It was the most heroic missions in the history of the United States. And truth is, it went wildly wrong.

Everybody wants to talk about the results of the mission, but it was their *preparation* that made it possible to handle their *oh-shit moment* in the most extreme conditions. Astronauts, UFC fighters, Navy SEALs, and so forth all prepare for the most extreme conditions, and they perform accordingly.

Good news for you: your life is not on the line. Whatever your cause might be or that "thing" you need to prepare for is far less risky. But what if you took the mentality of preparation—not only for the task at hand but also for plan B or even plans C, D, E, and F? What if something goes terribly wrong? Will you be comfortable in your own skin, or as my old mentor Ron used to say, "shit the sheets"?

A failure to plan is a plan for failure. If something is important enough to you, you will find time to prepare, physically and mentally.

On a personal note, I speak in hundreds of cities annually. Each day that I present, you will find me in the gym that morning. Why? Blood flow, endorphin release, and feeling physically fit enhance my performance. In my headphones, you would hear motivational videos or audio. Before getting ready for that day, I will not leave my hotel room without a fifteen-minute meditation.

These are the simple practices that can move the needle

from failure to success. Even if just a notch, it can be significant. Does it sound like too much for what you have going on?

Not if your American Dream 2.0 goals are big enough. Big goals require big preparation. And if you don't agree that these little things are necessary, you're mulling through life with a complacency for mediocracy.

Get bigger goals that require this preparation mindset.

Happy with your nine-to-five job, strolling in hungover, leaving early, turning on Netflix when you get home—all good. Just don't bitch about it or blow smoke that you've got the "next best discovery." Ideas are easy. Execution is a whole different ball game. Hard work and preparation are American Dream 1.0 mindsets that are as important, if not more important, today with the American Dream 2.0.

ACTION ITEMS

When NASA sent the first astronauts to the moon, much of their training focused on one thing: how to handle panic. This is their primary training!

They went through hundreds of simulations of all the things that could go wrong on their mission. The leaders of the space program were teaching those astronauts how to handle adversity—even the things they could not predict.

You don't have to fly a rocket to the moon or join the Navy SEALs to experience adversity. We all experience adversity every day.

It's how you handle that adversity that determines whether you'll achieve your American Dream 2.0. Winging it is not a plan. Mental preparation is.

PART 4

===

THE AMERICAN DREAM 2.0: *YOUR STORY*

CHAPTER 33

* * *

SOCIAL MEDIA: THE GIFT AND THE CURSE

Your uncle's nauseating political views? Your married friends—who you know are getting divorced—posting about their perfect relationship? Or the dog pics? Man, we get it already—you love your dog!

These are all things that might make us annoyed at that online space and social media.

Look, I understand. I empathize with your distaste of social media. I share it sometimes, too. In fact, let me be really honest. As much as I think it's a valuable platform, along with things like YouTube, Vimeo, and so on, I *rarely* scroll through it. #truth.

But don't let that annoyance keep you from taking advantage of it. This is the greatest opportunity in the history of humankind to be a marketer. In the American Dream 1.0, you had to spend thousands of dollars on print, mail, billboards, and so forth, and with no real way to measure your success.

And I don't mean just vomiting a bunch of posts on your feed. The accessible data to geotarget your audience is *insane*. Quick example: I laugh at businesses that just send spam email thinking that's marketing. Ten thousand emails, with a crappy newsletter at a 5 percent open rate. Perhaps come up with a *quality* list, put into the back end of Facebook, create look-alike audiences, and ensure your content shows up in front of them. Your "open rate" just sky-rocketed. Now do video and have people actually get to know *you*.

I talk a lot about social media when I speak to large audiences. It's just where people are, and if you're marketing and want to gain market share. It's just kinda dumb to chase mediums that are dead. So many romanticize about the past and refuse to accept the old ways of doing things as worthless.

I always ask, "How many of you in some way, shape, or form do something for your business or brand on social media? Raise your right hand."

Most of the right hands in the audience go up, including mine.

"Now, how many of you are *nauseated* by social media? Raise your left hand. It's okay for everyone in this room to have *both* of your hands up—I know I do!"

If social media platforms didn't also represent a significant portion of our commerce, I wouldn't give a rip about it, and that's the truth. I already have enough friends in real life. I don't need digital ones.

That being said, you'd be remiss to ignore the facts. We have the greatest opportunity in the history of humankind to connect with and influence other people for our cause, whether it be your charity, upcoming event, business idea, or whatever. You got a story? Want people to know about it on the masses? Door knocking ain't gonna get it done.

Did you ever imagine you could push a button on a phone and in two minutes have a driver pick you up in an Escalade?

Did you ever believe that people would meet their spouses online?

No matter how unlikely it seems, these are the times we live in. Go ahead and disregard the trend because social media is annoying. Or you can take some time to get to know all the mediums.

Now, granted you might only like social media as a means to keep up with friends, and scroll your feed from time to time. That's fine. To each their own.

But if you have a real purpose—a real cause or business you need to promote—social media is *the* platform to make it happen. For the first time ever, the Davids have as much power as the Goliaths in business.

It's your story. And if you're not doing outreach, *at least* have what people find about *you* represent you well. If your website is some manufactured cookie-cutter non-sense you didn't even create the content on, guess what? In today's world, that's already outdated and counterproductive. If it isn't vibrant with a story and video content, it's garbage.

Manufactured content you didn't create is worthless.

I know, sucks to read. You like your website, even spent some money on it. But you know I'm right. It gets stale quick. Fix it. Your newsletter—you don't even write it. Guess what? People know. You're annoying people by sending it.

As an example, Realtors who think it's "marketing" when the company they pay to send their automatic monthly newsletter gives the "Top 4 Tips on How to Clean Your Home This Spring." Recipient: click → spam.

For God's sake, if you can't come up with your own content, you shouldn't be in the business you call yourself an expert in. *Stop!*

Whether you like it or not, people Google you, and they sure as hell check out your social media pages. What do they find? What is your story?

The Salad Bowl—my father's cafeteria—they didn't have a social media page, and people didn't look them up on Yelp. These were the American Dream 1.0 days. They were around much earlier than that. But you know what? They had a story. People talked about them. They were known in "the neighborhood."

Today's "neighborhood" is significantly bigger. And it's a double-edged sword: it's an opportunity and a risk. The opportunity is the connectivity. The risk is that people can talk about you and your brand and spread some bad press quick. The expression, "There is no such thing as negative press..."

Um, yeah, that's not true—at all.

People emailing people asking their opinion of your product or service and having negative opinions...Bad press is bad. That's why it's called bad press.

The point is, now more than ever, if you have a cause, then your story matters. You have an opportunity to bring it to live in a way American Dream 1.0 companies like the Salad Bowl could never dream of.

The history of business goes like this. Mom-and-pop shops had a story known by the neighborhood. Big retailers crushed them, because they made things cheaper. The internet took out the retailers, because not only was it cheaper, but it was also quicker and easier. *Now* it's come full circle. The people (you) can disrupt the disruptors. Take the power back!

How?

Your story. It matters now more than ever. Just like the American Dream 1.0, except on a bigger scale. Truth is, technological innovations are like an avalanche, and it's coming for every industry in the world. You can either get snowed in by it, or you can hop on your snowboard and enjoy the ride. The choice is yours.

★ ★ ★

CHAPTER 34

YOUR BUTT WON'T PAY YOUR RENT

In every business, you have to strike a delicate balance between three elements:

- Content
- Revenue
- Value

Think of those elements like a triangle. At the top of the triangle is *content*. That's the fun part. That's your purpose, passion, and overall message.

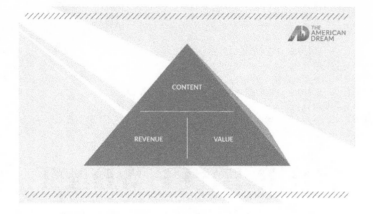

Your goal, as a servant thought leader, is to deliver *value* to those who engage with your content. That value you provide in turn may bring you opportunities to generate *revenue*, no matter what industry you're in. Let's give an example in the fitness industry.

Scroll through Instagram. There is no shortage of half-naked fitness junkies pretending they're high-paid protein shake spokespeople. Most of them are phony, with narcissistic content. In fact, you could say that about a lot of industries, online and off.

I know some very successful people in this space, and kudos to them for following their passion and turning it into a profit. Hell, if Kylie Jenner could make one post and suck $1.6 billion in value out of Snapchat, it's tough to argue with that kind of influence. That being said, most of us aren't supermodels.

But who cares about them. You might have a huge heart for animals; who's to say that can't be converted to a dog-walking business that you promote on Facebook? Or you're a mortgage professional and you leverage Instagram to create conversation about the neighborhoods you help people finance their real estate. Perhaps you have a charity near and dear to your heart that others have a passion for as well. Start a chat group.

Whatever your ambition, you can find your way in this space.

But back to those "fitness experts." Let's single them out (or at least the ones who do it wrong), because we've all seen them on our feeds by now. Here's where some of them actually get it right: the ones going to the gym at 5:00 a.m.—living by example. More importantly, giving us value—that is, nutrition tips, proper ways to exercise, showing *others* (not just themselves), and so forth.

That's their passion, and that's what they're inspired to do. Good for them!

But then there's that notorious half-naked selfie in the gym mirror posted to Instagram. It might get some likes, because *news flash*: people tend to like looking at half-naked bodies. Also, because there's a lot of creepers out there. But is there *any* value in that behavior? What does a bunch of likes really even mean anyway? Can't build a business with likes.

It's as shallow as a baby pool.

Look, don't get me wrong. Their dedication to get in that gym is great. But their selfie about it doesn't add value, and it certainly won't grow revenue. It will gain them a lot of followers, aka creepers, and likely get some likes, but likes won't pay your rent or, one day, your mortgage. A lot of followers means nothing. There is way more value in having quality followers, a tribe who truly likes you and your message, rather than a bunch of creeps.

Unfortunately, that's where a lot of entrepreneurs in every industry get it wrong with social media, not just fitness.

The life coaches are the next category. Nobody wants to be coached about life by an unemployed twenty-something-year-old. You know what teaches you about life? Um, *life*.

Have something of value to provide, or don't provide it all.

That old WIFM acronym: **What's in It for Me?**

No matter what business you're in—fitness, real estate, media, accounting, or just trying to promote your charity or spread a good word—social media success means being a thought leader and giving *value*. The narcissistic posts aren't providing insight, value, solutions, and so forth. They're just self-fulfilling.

Not to compare you to these folks, but it is important to be mindful yourself of the content you create. I'll be the first to admit, there are times when I get so fired up that I post a rant. Later when I go read it, I realize that if I were reading it or watching that video, who cares? Nobody is perfect at this thing, and it's just important we be self-aware.

WIFM is for your audience, not you. What's in it for them? What value are you providing? And sure, there are many times that it can just be entertainment value. Just don't get caught up in your own hype. We call that "being a legend in your own shower."

CHAPTER 35

* * *

WIFM!

Straight up: if you want to grow your cause or business and gain market share, you have to be a great marketer. Today, that's done in the way of video (your story), digital (getting it in front of people on the masses/internet), and social (getting good word spread about you). But just like the American Dream 1.0, relationships are always a key ingredient.

It starts with gaining the attention of your ideal demographic. Most of us in business have a purpose—that's our drive. But let's be honest, we also want to make money. I'm always supersensitive to the money topic, because I never want to be confused for the clowns out there who make it *all about the money*. Rollin' up on Instagram in cars they don't own. Or hell, even if they do, so what? That ain't me.

But you know who they are. The tool in front of his Lamborghini telling you how rich he is, and if you sign up for his program, he'll make you rich, too. Makes me ill.

But sure, you want to monetize your passion—I get it—as you should. Nothing wrong with that. That's just how it works, but you can monetize your passion without selling out. I am a huge believer that if you follow your true purpose, the revenue will follow.

Selling out is what mainstream media does. Do the opposite of them. Lead people to something positive. If you're a fitness guru, nobody cares about your selfies. If you're a financial professional, nobody cares how much money you have.

If you're a "life coach," make your social media posts about the end-all user's life, not yours.

Of course, personal stories can be good—they make you relatable—but when you find yourself talking about yourself too much, nobody cares.

WIFM—"What's in it for me?"

If you're afraid of giving away your best content for free, guess what? You're stuck in the American Dream 1.0. That's a scarcity mindset, and it doesn't fly in the American Dream 2.0. Live in an abundance mindset. Give your content away, and don't fear being copied either. I fear the day I stop being copied, and so should you.

THE DELICATE BALANCE OF SOCIAL MEDIA

Owning a media company (Instagram @craigsewing-media) and creating a national TV show, *The American Dream* (@theamericandreamtv) has taught me a few things. One of them is the delicate balance between revenue and content.

Content is the fun part. But without revenue, good luck growing your company. If you focus on only the revenue, you're an infomercial. Walking that fine line is a delicate dance.

Focus on your end-all customer, give away great content and value, and when it comes to how you make your money (aka your "call to action"), weave it in seamlessly and don't make it your primary objective. Money will follow a great purpose, I promise!

CHAPTER 36

* * *

MAN VERSUS ROBOT

Uber is the number one taxicab company that doesn't own a car. Airbnb is the number one hotel chain that doesn't own a hotel. If you do not believe technology is coming for your industry, your head is in the sand.

I love referencing the real estate industry as a prime example of the vast technological advancement happening in society. Granted I'm a little biased, as it's my background, but it's such an important part of life; it speaks to the big picture of the American Dream 2.0.

Look, you need food, water, and shelter. Real estate is a core component, whether you're in the industry. You gotta live somewhere.

In real estate, businesses like Redfin, Purple Brick, and others in this sector have made it clear that they want to circumvent the Realtor, more specifically, the commission. Automation is happening in every industry. The Zillows of the world want to facilitate the home shopping process. Well, let's be honest, they also want to make a boatload of money doing it, too. Can't really argue with that in a free marketplace.

There is certainly a sliver of the market that would like this transactional-based model of buying a home. The reality of real estate and other industries is that *you cannot automate relationships*. My parents still live in the house I was raised in, and there is no online platform that can communicate *the story* of that neighborhood better than they can, with the help of a human.

> And if any industry needs a shake-up, it's the real estate industry. In 2008, there was a market crash, and real estate lobbyists protected that profession, while others got crushed.

In the past, I've owned real estate and mortgage companies, but that's as a business owner. As an everyday American, even with my knowledge in the space, I realize the importance of a serious professional. Serious is a key word, as it takes longer to get your hairstyling license than your real estate license, so they are plenty of jokers in this space.

And let's go even more old school. When I refer to my

parents still living in the house I was raised in, it was a real relationship that guided them into what ultimately became the neighborhood they'd raise their family and made their friendships. That was then, this is now. And still not much has changed.

The truth is, new first-time homebuyers still want that relationship. Many refer to buying a home as the "American dream." I certainly think it can be a piece of it. It's not only a home; it's also one's biggest investment. Even in the American Dream 2.0, the human being is irreplaceable.

Whatever industry you're in, do not fear technology. Earlier, I mentioned Uber and Airbnb. Look at Amazon, too. Amazon was the number one retailer that didn't own a store. Well, that is until they did.

They spent a whole bunch of money on studying consumer behavior learning that people may shop online, but they still like to buy in person. Now Amazon owns bookstores. Go figure!

While technology grows, so should your confidence. Automation will suffocate your competition but not you. Ultimately, nobody will ever figure out a way to automate a handshake or a hug. Those who will succeed in the American Dream 2.0 will not fear technology; they will embrace it, leverage it, and use it to their advantage.

Humans win.

SPEAKING OF HOMEOWNERSHIP...

Buy your own home and pay your own mortgage rather than paying *your landlord's* mortgage.

This will always be true for the American dream. You can invent only so much dirt. There is no greater investment on earth than...*earth*. We're not making any more of it anytime soon. Make buying a home part of your financial goals.

CHAPTER 37

★ ★ ★

CONNECTING THE DISCONNECTED

I am a firm believer that we are the most connected disconnected people in the history of the planet. The noisier the online world gets and artificial intelligence we develop, the more important human stories will be. It's time to double down on human beings.

The media would have you believe that people are becoming less important; after all, drivers, doctors, lawyers, real estate agents, and even grocery stores are all being phased out due to technological advances. Isn't that proof positive that technology is more important than humans?

The technological advances in all industries are fascinating, but it doesn't change the fact people connect with people.

All of us are still in this thing together, and we like good stories and the opportunity to support others. I highly doubt the "machines" will take over anytime soon—or as sci-fi movies would make you believe, kill us all. At least I hope not, but if that happens, you got bigger problems than a misanalysis from this book.

In the American Dream 2.0, people continue to yearn for the real story. The modern-day medium for which they are shared has just changed dramatically. No matter what business you're in, you have to be known for something. And in order to be known for something, you must have a story.

Marketing is what gets people to you. Brand is what they find once they get there. Your story is your brand.

Look at the old American Dream 1.0 way of telling your story.

You put up a billboard or bought an ad in the newspaper, and you *expected* people to contact you with their business. But through those mediums, you didn't provide anyone with real value. You asked for only value in return, and you asked it on a dying medium.

Billboards? Print advertising? Commercials? They offer little to no story—at least not something that can be followed.

In the American Dream 2.0, the mediums are video, digital, and social, and just like the American Dream 1.0, always relational. The truth is, we have a collective case of ADD, and it's not just the kids, but it's the adults, too. We have an addiction to constant stimulation. My wish for you is to be cognizant of your own addictions and be able to unplug when you need to. We are all guilty of being too connected to technology at times.

Next time you get on an elevator, try looking around you. Notice something about all the people around you. They're likely on their phone. They are more interested in their phone than anyone else. This is where we are at. Deny it, or realize that's where people's attention is. And if you are to successfully market to the masses, you need to go where the eyeballs are.

That's the world we live in.

On the brighter side, a big part of that desire for stimulation is also a desire to share *genuine* stories. In such a phony world, people want stories they can relate to. In fact, authenticity and imperfection are two of the most important ingredients to a good story in the American Dream 2.0.

In the American Dream 1.0, your story reached only your tiny neighborhood where you had limited connectivity and fewer options to connect. Just like at the Salad Bowl, people knew the stories of those mom-and-pop shops, because they knew the people who ran them. Communities were the neighborhoods the brick and mortar sat in.

Now, in the American Dream 2.0, you have way more connectivity, the neighborhood lives online, it's significantly bigger, and people can talk, share, and connect online. This is where *brands* live and die.

But one fact remains the same: people want authenticity.

And because there are so many options to share your story, you have to tailor it for each medium.

- On Instagram, your image or video is the key (people are less likely to read a long caption).
- On Facebook, people expect to read more, so writing a long post makes more sense.
- With Twitter, you have no choice but to make it short.
- On YouTube or Vimeo, you'll benefit with videos that get to the point quickly.

But no matter where you share your story, your main concern should be your authenticity, and your audience.

The future will be full of AI and robots, and yeah, some of them will take our jobs. But the more automated and *artificially* intelligent the world becomes, the more we'll yearn for human connection. And the best way to connect is through stories.

CHAPTER 38

* * *

THE BLUE OCEAN STRATEGY

Compete where your competitors aren't.

This is the concept behind one of the best business books ever written, *Blue Ocean Strategy* by Renée Mauborgne and W. Chan Kim:

> The common mistake people make is they think that the way to succeed is to outwork, outcompete, and outspend others in their space. In some cases that can be true—I'll never knock hard work—however, think about how you can create a paradigm shift.

Compete where your competitors aren't.

Remember, I was in the mortgage banking industry when we went into radio. Why did we do that? Because radio was a differentiator for us. It made us different, it got people talking, and way more importantly, we leveraged the show to add value to others, inviting them onto the program and sharing their story. Building relationships!

The radio show was how we created content. Today, there are many, many more platforms to do something similar—and inexpensively, too. You can start a podcast, blog, or YouTube channel at this very moment for *free*. All of this comes from the necessity to create content.

How can *you* create a paradigm shift in your business?

ACTION ITEMS

- Write out all the things you do to compete with people in business.

- What are they doing?

- How are they spending?

- How are they building relationships and brand?

- How can you do something completely different to accomplish your goal of gaining market share?

Think outside of the box.

We ran a mortgage company and were able to change the game because we started a radio show. What can you do? What's your blue ocean strategy?

CHAPTER 39

★ ★ ★

SCUBA DIVER MARKETING

Back in those mortgage banking days, my business partner and I spent hundreds of thousands of dollars on mail marketing—a whole bunch of marketing money to get our message into your physical mailbox!

We would ship those mailers off all over the country. Then, because it was snail mail, we'd wait by the phones like we were watching paint dry, hoping for a call.

At first, this strategy worked really well because we had a good system around it. Mail is a dying medium, but the system we used still works today. We called it the Customer Journey.

Here's how our marketing plan worked (and yes, it's still

a good plan for today's American Dream 2.0). I'll do a direct comparison between:

American Dream 1.0—Mail
and
American Dream 2.0—Email

WHO?

1.0: It started with a list: *Who* were our prospects? In other words, whose mailbox did we want our marketing to wind up in?

2.0: In today's environment, that might be your email list. Are you just spamming the crap out of everyone (which is annoying, counterproductive, and illegal), or are you truly targeting your ideal demographic?

HOW?

1.0: Once our piece reached the mailboxes, *how* did we make sure they opened it?

The same is true today. If you're like me, you check your mailbox once a week. You get this big pile of mail, then you sort it out into two piles: what's junk and what's real. True, right?

Well, we had to make sure people opened our piece. Our design looked like a W-2 form. We had the word *confidential* written on it in red. Nothing wrong, illegal, unethical, or dishonest about that. We just made it look like something they'd put in the *real* pile, not the *junk* pile.

2.0: In today's environment, your hook could be as simple as a good subject line in your email, or the first sentence of a post, or video. It *kills* me how much people go right for the jugular right in the beginning. You have to lead them down a path.

WHAT?

1.0: With our mail piece, our goal was to get potential customers to call us. So we kept it short, sweet, enticing, and never thought about our end goal other than to take them to the next step. For us, that was a call to our firm. *Just a call* was our objective.

2.0: In today's environment, ease back on your mile-long emails that nobody reads and just focus on what encourages them to take the next step. Some of the best emails are simply one to two sentences.

All of this is very simple. Yet, as the world kept turning, the one thing that stayed constant was change, and we saw that change in the most painful of ways.

Imagine dropping a huge spend on a mail piece and waiting for that phone to ring—only to find yourself weeks in the future, hearing nothing but silence!

Did the mail company actually deliver our materials?

Was our messaging off?

Did we try to reach the wrong people?

But if we didn't get calls, all we knew for certain was that our piece *bombed* and we were out a whole lot of money because of it. As you can imagine, it doesn't take many of these failures before you're suddenly in debt. Our direct mail marketing was an American dream 1.0 solution.

Whereas in the American Dream 2.0, your online marketing investments give you exact measurements of clicks, views, demographics, and location. You get measurable results, and you can figure out exactly what works, what doesn't, and *why. It's the equivalent of a scuba diver taking the worm directly to the fish's mouth!*

In the American Dream 1.0 world, you just stare at the phone and pray it rings.

With the American Dream 2.0, you have way more options, they're way less expensive, and you have a whole bunch of data that can support or deny your marketing decisions. Facebook is single-handedly the best platform I have ever seen for marketing. You can build audiences, target them, and ensure your content shows up in front of them. And truth be told, all social medias have value for gaining market share.

CHAPTER 40

* * *

"YOU" MESSAGING

Nothing we did worked.

A sponsor of our radio show owned a business that helped people improve their credit scores. This was in 2009, when people really needed help with this (still do). But nobody responded to our endorsements.

What was the problem?

I learned this lesson *first* by learning how to truly *engage* an audience, which in turn *grew* the audience and made our endorsements that much more valuable. But when we started this show in San Diego, we went about it *all wrong*. Like everyone, I'd been communicating since I was a child, so naturally this should be easy, right?

Not quite. I sucked.

But when I learned the power of *you*, everything changed. What I learned was that even though people might listen to a radio show as a large audience, they don't listen *together*. They were separately driving in their cars or listening by themselves on their headphones.

This realization created a subtle shift in how I communicated. For example, I realized I'd been opening our show all wrong:

WRONG: "Hey, *San Diego*, welcome to the show. Thank you, *everyone*, for being here."

I was speaking to the masses rather than the individual, and it was disengaging.

RIGHT: "Hello, thank *you* for tuning in. Got a great show for *you* today."

Can you see the difference? If you've ever studied neuro-linguistic programming (NLP), you might be familiar with how speaking to one person, even if there is an audience, is way more effective. In the first example, I'm talking to an entire city and using words like *everyone*.

In the second example, I am speaking to *one* person. When I learned this, I experienced major growth in my audience. Thanks to our *you* messaging.

Now, back to that sponsor I was referring to earlier, the one with the credit business. Because he was a partner and he was a cool guy, we wanted to do everything in our power to get him more business.

What I realized was that I wasn't using *you* messaging in the endorsements of his practice. While we made this realization for a radio show back in 2009, *you* messaging is still incredibly valuable in our content-driven world, especially if you're creating videos for your passion. Videos should be created speaking to *one* person at a time.

As an example, which of these greetings is more engaging and personalized?

"Hey, everyone. We've got a sponsor who has this cool credit score improvement kit he's offering everyone in our audience."

Or:

"Thank you for tuning in. I have something very cool to share with you. Do you have credit issues like so many people right now?

"As one of our valued listeners, you have the opportunity to get a free gift from one of our partners. We've known him for years, and now is such a great time for this offer.

"Imagine this: you reach into your pocket and pull out your phone right now. You simply send a text message to 74479 for a free credit package. In response, you'll get a text back with a link, which you can follow to receive your free credit improvement package.

"Now imagine the confidence you'll feel when you get home to your spouse and explain how you'll raise your credit to 750 or higher. Imagine the sense of security and comfort you can give her knowing that you can achieve optimal financing because you have great credit."

These changes made dramatic improvements to our endorsement and brought value to our partner. Allow me to elaborate further.

Not only should you tailor your content to *you* messaging, but rather than speaking to large audiences, you should practice eliminating *I*, *we*, and *me* from your content as well.

Not an easy thing to do and not something you can do 100 percent of the time. But by replacing *I*, *we*, or *me* with you framework, it'll cause your message to penetrate better.

As an example, let's say you were a financial advisor and giving a video market update for your newsletter and social media.

WRONG: Hi, on *my* video today, I am going to talk about how the Federal Reserve raised interest rates, and I'll share why this is going to hurt the market and investors."

RIGHT: Hi, thank *you* for watching this video. Today, *you* will hear me discuss how the Federal Reserve raised interest rates, and *you* will learn the best strategies to navigate this market and protect *your* assets.

Cut much of the *I*, *we*, and *me*. Reframe it as *you*. It's more engaging!

ACTION ITEMS

It doesn't matter what business you're in or what message you're getting out there. If you create content of any kind, you can use these techniques. It's not some Jedi mind trick bullshit meant to dupe anybody. It's simply focusing on the person you are looking to serve more effectively.

Videos, blogs, tweets, or even speaking to an audience the old-school way—if you engage your audience's emotions, tell good stories, and use *you* messaging, you will create much more engaging content and better results.

CHAPTER 41

* * *

YOUR "NOT TO DO" LIST

For some reason, they gave us a sword.

It was 2007, and my business partner and I had just won the award for top performing branch in Benchmark Mortgage out of 314 nationwide.

The keynote speaker at the event was Todd Duncan, a best-selling author of *Life on a Wire*, among many other books. Todd pulled me aside after the event. "Come out to my office in La Jolla. Let's get to know each other better. I want to know what you guys are doing that nobody else in this room is."

We obliged.

Unfortunately, despite winning the award, I knew that we were on a transactional treadmill: we spent a boatload on marketing, only to chase that marketing nut each month.

Did we win first place? Sure. But we were up a ladder on the wrong wall, and we knew it.

Slaves to our overhead. We essentially ran a transaction-based business fielding inbound calls from our outgoing mail bombs: we had zero relationships with our clients and never even saw them face-to-face.

We knew what we were doing was not sustainable, but we didn't know any other way. You ever see a UFC fighter get his ass kicked in the ring but was so tough he just wouldn't go down, only to his own detriment? You're shouting at the screen like, "C'mon, man, stop taking the beating. Go down!"

That was us; we were hustling ourselves to death. We worked long hours, spent big, and had no referral relationships, but we were forced to hustle to keep up with the business we trapped ourselves in.

Maybe Todd, this stranger we only knew from a single event as a keynote speaker, could give us some advice. The next week, we went to his office overlooking the Pacific Ocean.

It had floor-to-ceiling windows overlooking all of La Jolla Cove, with surfers cutting through waves. It was early in the morning, and there was a full moon sitting over the edge of the coast. Picturesque!

"Look at that," Todd said, pointing out on the water. "That's what I call a moon rise."

Todd asked us some questions.

We did our best to sound legit and look cool, but when you're sitting with a legend, it's not easy to pretend.

Todd kept prying into our company. I knew where he was going: he was looking for our pain points. I tried to play it cool in my responses.

With every question, I felt like a ten-year-old covering his mouth, trying to hold back a secret. Then it happened. Simply put, my business partner lost his shit.

I don't remember the question. I just remember him having what I can only describe as a conniption fit. He exploded!

He said, "I don't even know where to start!

"Every month, we spend tons of money, sometimes

$50,000 to $100,000, to get all these leads—and we are closing them—but we're burning the candle at both ends. The moment our marketing doesn't work, we're screwed. We'll have credit card debt, our vendors will hate us, and we'll be out on our ass. We have a lot of people making money on us right now, but the market's gonna turn one of these days. And when it does, all of those people will be *losing* money on us. And meanwhile, look over there." He pointed out the window. "Out there is a money train— *Choooo! Choooo!*—and everybody else is on it, while we're stuck in this black hole trying to climb our way out!"

I swear he didn't even breathe.

Meanwhile, I was staring a hole in his head like, "Dude, chill out!" But he ran right through all of my stop signs. I could've been standing there waving flares like Nicholas Cage at the end of *The Rock* and he still wouldn't have noticed.

When he finally stopped, you could hear a pin drop. After a few moments passed (which felt like an eternity), Todd looked at me and said one word: "Whoa."

A tiny smile crept across his face, and I couldn't help but laugh. Then the two of us started cracking up hysterically. It was so damn funny to see this cool and collected guy firehouse a best-selling author and world-renowned speaker.

Todd said, "Well, guys, breakdowns lead to break-throughs. And *that* was a breakdown."

He then gave us an old-school American Dream 1.0 time management strategy.

He said, "Next week, I want you to time block everything you do in five-minute increments. I don't care if you're sending faxes, going to the bathroom, or making calls. If you do something in the next week, I want you to write it down. Period.

"Once you get that all written out, you'll have a list of activities that can fit in two categories: things that actually produce revenue for your company and things that don't. Highlight revenue-producing activities in green, and highlight non-revenue-producing activities in orange. Then why don't you boys come back here next week and show me what you find."

When we did that for the following week, we found something troubling: only 20 percent of our activities were highlighted in green, meaning 80 percent of our time was *not* spent on revenue-generating activities.

When we went back to La Jolla to see him, he looked over our sheets of time tracking.

"How much money do you two want to make? Imagine how much you'd make if 80 percent of your activities were green instead of orange. You need to find support people you currently work with to do the orange activities and take them off your plate."

"We can't hire more people," I said. "Our monthly expenses are already through the roof."

Todd gave us a serious look. "You can't afford not to.

"You might look at a new hire as overhead, but it's not. A good doctor is nothing without a nurse. The nurse gets everything prepared so the doctor can come in and give a quicker diagnosis. Restaurant owners don't flip burgers either.

"Look, you guys are talented; there's no question about that. You're so talented that you can do anything in your business. Don't. Your time is better spent on bigger revenue-producing activities. Hiring other people to send faxes and grab lunch frees up your time to do more important activities."

Todd's advice totally changed the way we viewed our

time. This was a game changer—just the perspective alone. And one thing I've truly learned since then...

When you make the decision to spend on your own growth, whether it be school, training, seminars, that bigger office, hiring staff, or whatever, the moment you make that decision is the moment you feel inspiration in your heart to act on it. Put your own feet to the fire. You don't make decisions and then let yourself down after the fact. Investing in your growth is the very best thing you can do, even though sometimes it's the hardest.

It's that paralysis by analysis that freezes all of us. You have to break the pattern, and sometimes that means decisions that *force* success onto yourself.

Look at your own life.

Let's talk a bit about generating an income for your business. Again, I'm sensitive to this topic because I never want to be remembered as the guy touting how much money you can make. It ain't my brand, and there are too many clowns talking about this in the American Dream 2.0. This is strictly to give you some sound advice around growing your income.

And look, if you have a serious passion, you can turn that purpose into an income. And none of us want to be broke.

But enough with the disclaimers. Let's talk about it for a moment. As far as I'm concerned, money is just a scoreboard. You can use it as a good way to analyze if you're growing (and of course, it has some perks, too).

So here's my question:

How much money do you want to make a year?

Is it $50,000?

$100,000?

$250,000?

$1,000,000?

$5,000,000?

The answer to that one is up to you. My advice: whatever you want to make, 10x it, and let that be how you think. That's what Grant Cardone would tell you to do. Think *big*.

Let's use an example that put in the top 1 percent of income earners. Let's say someone wanted to make $250,000 a year for the following example here: With forty hours per work week, and forty-eight work weeks a year (with holidays), that makes 1,920 work hours per year. That means in order to make $250,000 a year, you have to earn $130 per hour, plus or minus.

You could do this same math with *any* income you desire.

Now look at your own daily activities.

If you spent an hour of your week doing administrative tasks, is that a good use of your time? Well, to find the answer, ask yourself this question:

Would you pay somebody $130 an hour to do that task for you?

The answer is likely no. If you weren't willing to pay someone else to do work for that amount, you are essentially robbing yourself. It's a great litmus test to measure whether your activities are the highest and best use of your time.

Time is your most valuable asset. And the truth is, there is plenty of it to pursue your passion, even if it's a side hustle to your day job. That's what the current American dream landscape offers you: an opportunity to earn your income *and* grow your dream—or when the time is right, to go *all in*.

When someone says, "I don't have enough time," it's the

biggest bullshit excuse in the world. You have *plenty* of time. There is no exception to that statement. You sleep eight hours a day? Start sleeping six. Boom! You just added two hours a day, fourteen hours a week = *a full day* added to each week.

Is there an hour a day you waste on social media? Maybe more?

It's one thing if you are on the smartphone for work, but it's another thing if it's an addiction. Cut that out, and you just got back an hour-plus per day. Time is the most precious asset we have. Be conscious of how you invest it.

Old-school time management is timeless, not only in yesterday's American Dream 1.0. It's equally as important in the American Dream 2.0. In fact, the American Dream 2.0 has plenty of time management apps you could download right onto your smartphone.

Through Todd Duncan's exercise, we quickly hired out as many orange-highlighted activities as possible and spent 80 percent of our time on revenue-generating activities. What we learned was invaluable:

Almost all of the green-highlighted activities were related to *relationship building.*

We saw clearly that the only way to survive the inevitable crash was by being less transactional and being more relational. That was how we got on the "money train" my partner freaked out about for our business.

I'm still not sure why he pointed out that window as if there was a train choo-chooing through the Pacific Ocean, but I'm glad he did.

Breakdowns do lead to breakthroughs. We soon converted our business, through good old-fashioned time management, to be a relationship-oriented business, hopping off the transactional treadmill.

ACTION ITEMS

- Where are you wasting time?

- Where do you feel stuck in paralysis by analysis?

- Where could your day be filled with more green highlighter time blocks?

What doesn't get measured doesn't get done. Try the time-blocking challenge to see how you can maximize the most important asset of your day: your time.

CHAPTER 42

★ ★ ★

BUSINESS OR BUSYNESS

Is it a device, or is it an addiction?

Only you can answer that question, but that little thing in your pocket called a smartphone is the most powerful invention in the history of humankind. It also creates an incredible opportunity. Personally, I run multiple businesses, including a media company.

We have a nice office, but I am rarely there. It is way more important for me to be other places building relationships. Truth is, because of my smartphone I am able to connect to people, learn, check email, socialize, market, and so on and so forth. The list is a mile long.

And I can do it all remotely! Often, I take Ubers rather

than drive my own car, just so I can be free to make calls and check emails. But that device can also be dangerous, especially for kids growing up today who were born with an iPad as a babysitter and don't know any better.

I love inspiring entrepreneurs, so let's focus on that group. But much of this applies to anything you are inspired to accomplish. There is a big difference between business and busyness.

The latter confuses motion with action.

Busyness means hiding behind your computer, scrolling through nonsense, and posting content without building any real relationships.

Business is leveraging these platforms to engage people in a way that older generations in American Dream 1.0 business people only dreamed of.

You might have valid objections against social media.

I get it. You might say, "I know it's good for my business, but the truth is, I can't stand it. I hate reading the views of annoying people." It's perfectly valid to call social media nauseating. I actually agree with you. But for old-school people who find it annoying, it's two simple steps:

1. Unfollow annoying people.
2. Don't be annoying.

Done.

Using social media for business looks like this: you connect with people online *and you follow through to build a relationship offline.*

One of the best practitioners of this is Seth O'Byrne in San Diego, who is now the star of a TV show called *Hot Properties* on HGTV. He's one of the top-producing Realtors in the market. He does more than $100 million in business each year. One day, he shared with me that he closed $5.2 million in real estate listings in one day.

"Guess where it came from?" he said. "Instagram."

He uses Instagram to post stories and engage his audience. As a result, he closes *real* business from it.

Please note: Instagram is *free.*

In the American Dream 1.0, you had to buy billboards, radio ads, print pieces, and commercials, all of which were *wildly* expensive and yielded random results. Today, connectivity is *free.*

And if you dive into paid advertising on social media, the intel and stats you can extract are incredible.

ACTION ITEMS

- Your parents didn't have these connection opportunities.

- Use them wisely—for business, not busyness.

- Again, unfollow annoying people, and don't be annoying. You'll feel much better about the whole thing.

CHAPTER 43

★ ★ ★

FIREBALL!

There is a cursed building at the corner of Market Street and Eighth Avenue in downtown San Diego. It's a prime piece of real estate, just blocks from Petco Park, where the San Diego Padres play their home games. If location is as important in real estate as they say it is, this should be one of the best spots in the city.

With constant foot traffic in the area, it's almost as if success would be forced upon it with a natural influx of customers. But every bar that sets up there dies almost as quickly as it was opened.

Then in 2011 came Errol Asuncion, Brendan Huffman, and more of the most-loved and highly respected people in the San Diego bar and restaurant scene. Errol specifically is the equivalent of the Energizer bunny. Some people collect stamps, baseball cards, or whatever.

This man collects relationships. *Everybody* knows Errol, and he's one of the most likable guys on the planet. They bought this cursed corner and started renovations on the building. The writing on the wall for failure was there before they even sold their first beer.

At least that's what people thought.

As the construction crew ripped the building down to the studs, Errol and his partners rolled up their sleeves and grinded with the construction team into the late-night hours.

They were no dummies. They knew this was a cursed corner, and their hope was they could do something different. That's when they heard it: the sirens.

There was a fire station just two blocks away, and every hour there was another fire truck zooming by with its lights flashing and sirens blaring. Maybe that's why this place was cursed—the damn fire trucks. They caused an obnoxious sound that ripped through the brick building all day and night.

So as the guys worked into late hours, they made drinking games to give themselves some form of entertainment while working their tails off.

Every time one of those obnoxious sirens blazed through the streets of San Diego, they would take a shot of Fireball, a new whiskey on the market.

What started as just a fun idea for a few guys hanging out became one of the best marketing strategies in bar history. This game became a staple of the bar now called Bootlegger.

Their bar is now one of the biggest sellers of Fireball whiskey in the entire country, and the locals call this bar the "Cheers of San Diego."

What used to be an obnoxious sound and an eyesore— sirens and lights flying by all day—is now a big reason why they're so successful.

Isn't it funny how just having a little fun during a state of annoyance can be a game changer? I think my mother, Julie Sewing, used to call this "turning lemons into lemonade."

ACTION ITEMS

- What curses in your life could be blessings with just a little shift in thinking?

- Maybe that frustration could be the first spark to your own Fireball story.

CHAPTER 44

* * *

HATERS GONNA HATE

The more content you create, the more people will hate on you. That's the circle of life on the internet. A lot of tough mofos sit behind their computer screens these days; as Jay-Z once said, they "wouldn't bust a grape in a fruit fight."

On that note, in 2018, I was asked to speak at an event in Seattle, put on by another media company. Sure, why not. Seattle's a fun town, and this looked like a cool event. Not too large but still about a thousand people in attendance.

The man behind the event had a back-end business that sold video products. He wanted to bring value to his audience on how to best leverage video as an asset. He invited me on stage for an interview on the topic. There was a long stretched-out couch on stage, so I jokingly put my feet up, and the interview started.

He said, "A lot of people I work with should be doing video, but they're nervous on camera. Craig, you're a national TV host and you train others in marketing. What advice can you give to those who are so nervous that they're reluctant to do video?"

I looked at the audience and said, "Just drink."

It got some chuckles.

Then I said, "You were nervous the first time you had sex, too, but you figured that out, right?"

More laughs.

But then I got serious, because I had a serious point to make.

"So many of us, including myself, get into our own heads to our own detriment.

"Personally, I am an introvert, and I *hated* public speaking when I started. But I hated being fearful even more. Growth comes from discomfort, and you have to be willing to beat your fears."

As for the Seattle audience, I refused to let anyone in that audience suffocate their dreams because of fear. So I leaned forward on that couch and looked at the audience.

"I have three rules for you. Ready?

"The first rule is: *Get out of your head and into your heart.* Period.

"When you're in your head, your subconscious takes over in some weird way and takes you away from your true intentions. You second-guess everything and make yourself a nervous wreck. Get into your heart! Speak from a place of love and compassion. So rule number one is *get out of your head and into your heart.*

"The second rule is: *Make it about them, not you.* Stop thinking all about you, how you look or sound, and whatever your desired result is.

"Focus on what gives your audience value. So rule number two is *make it about them, not you.*

"Rule number three is a summary of one and two.

"If you're out of your head and speaking from your heart; if you're making it about them, not you, then my third rule is this: for those who don't like you and your positive intentions—pardon my language—*fuck 'em.*"

It created a stir in the audience, which was a great moment, but I was also dead serious. Not everybody is going to love the things you have to say or the message you put out there. That's an impossible feat. You cannot let the haters be the focus of your decisions. If someone doesn't like your message, when your goal was to add value, and it came from the heart, is that someone you need to care about?

And this doesn't only apply to some stranger on the internet; this could be a friend, family member, or even a spouse. *Nobody* has the right to suffocate *your dream.* Often it's their own insecurities that create this.

Don't get me wrong, sometimes people you care about will have to give you constructive criticism, which maybe you don't want to hear. Always be self-aware and willing to make adjustments to become a better person. But there is a fine line between that and someone trying to rain on your parade.

If you are well-intentioned and have a big heart, then steamroll the critics. Do not let their insecurities mess with your mindset. You have too much to do in your life to worry about the haters.

If someone wants to hate on you, let that be their issue, not yours! Haters gonna hate, especially when it's easy to hide behind a computer these days. You have to focus on those who appreciate you. Period.

ACTION ITEMS

- Who in your life is a hater?

- Are there people holding you back who you need to cut out of your life?

- Are there people you need to set straight?

There is no time for negativity in the American Dream 2.0, no matter where it comes from. If you have haters, cut 'em loose.

Before you stop any activity because you're worried about haters, ask yourself:

- Is this hypothetical hater ever going to do business with me?

- Is that person ever going to be my friend?

If not, who gives a rip what they think about you? So many people get caught up worrying about haters that they don't follow through on all kinds of beneficial activities, such as creating content, and getting their message out to the world. Fears of being judged are the ultimate dream killers.

Look, I don't have to tell you that the internet is full of phonies. People can sniff bullshit better than ever. The moment you start manufacturing your content specifically to avoid haters, you'll not only neuter your content, but you'll also stress yourself out.

Everyone can sense inauthenticity, not just the haters.

When you first start creating content, the best thing you can do is allow yourself to be bad at it. That's authentic.

Being overly polished is not authentic. Perfectly scripted video creators, for example, sound like politicians. And people are sick of politicians. There's nothing inspiring about watching someone read from a script.

Speaking from the heart, though—now, *that's* inspiring. And guess what that opens you up to? Missteps and failures.

Be *radically authentic.*

And gladly welcome the haters; they mean you're doing something right.

And if you're really good, you'll see them convert and start copying you. That's when you know you're winning.

CONCLUSION

NEVER EVER SETTLE

The one thing you can count on is the world never stops turning. Sun goes up, sun goes down. Tide rolls in, tide rolls out. Every day, it keeps moving forward, and every day you have the opportunity to start anew. God is incredibly consistent this way. However, as the world turns, the one thing you can also count on is change. It gives us the opportunity to view life as a natural progression of seasons, one that brings new people and circumstances.

As you make your way through each season of your life, you'll encounter all kinds of individuals and groups you didn't know yesterday. Some of them you'll build lifelong relationships with, some of them you'll never see again, and everything in between.

Relationships are like trees, having leaves, branches, and the roots. Leaves are there for a season, and they can be beautiful for a short time. Same with acquaintances. Branches hold longer, but even they break off at some point, as do even good relationships. Your best relationships are like the roots of that tree: they'll be there forever.

If you're lucky, you'll find those the unique relationships that make you way more of a person than you would have ever been without them. These are the ones you confide in until the day you die. They're the people you can't outgrow, because you grow *with* each other.

The American Dream 1.0 and the American Dream 2.0—that will never change. This book has been premised on *relationships*.

Friends, acquaintances, communities, business partnerships, family, and if you're really lucky, your significant other. For me, that's my wife, Randee Sewing. She is the love of my life, and our relationship is the result of the most important lesson I can give you in this book:

Never settle.

That goes for anything. When launching and building our show *The American Dream,* I went old school. I traveled to different cities, funding my own face-to-face meetings with potential partners across the country. Even though we did leverage the online world of technology, I didn't hide behind a computer screen. Relationships are built in person.

In the early stages of the show, I traveled to all these cities and found myself in Denver.

Just by chance, I met Randee. Some call it love at first sight; I called it love at first vision, because I'd envisioned and dreamed of this girl my whole life. Nothing this profound can be made to pretend about or forced to settle upon.

As we dated in the craziest of ways, traveling all over the country, we could have let the long distance affect us and get in the way. After all, she lived in Denver and I lived in San Diego. We had every excuse in the world for this to not work, but when you have a purpose, anything seems possible. There is no purpose in the universe stronger than love.

As I jetted across the country launching our show, I flew Randee with me to almost every city. While I built the show *The American Dream*, I was building my own American dream, too.

For years before her, people told me to settle down and

find a wife. In fact, I even put this pressure on myself, wondering if I'd ever meet the right person. I could have given in to societal standards and married for the wrong reason sooner. But like anything, my inspiration for something greater far outweighed the notion of just settling. This goes for everything.

The American Dream 1.0 says that you're supposed to buy a house, get settled young, and spend the rest of your life rooted in the same spot, in many cases, building someone else's dream. To each their own, and this can be a perfectly happy life.

But the American Dream 2.0 gives you the opportunity to never settle.

It's about discovering your passion, creating your own reality, and finding your true love—whether that love is in a relationship, your work, a charity, or whatever purpose that drives you—or all of the above. It starts at its core, with love.

Don't settle for anything in life.

Never ever settle.

Strive for the people you love and the enjoyment you can't live without.

* * *

My parents are great people. They've been together since 1969 when they went on their first date on Valentine's Day. By the end of that June, they were engaged. They still live in the same house I was raised in, and they've had successful, meaningful lives. That is their American dream and an honorable one.

I went about things differently, as have many people living the American Dream 2.0. I've been a serial entrepreneur, lived in different places, traveled the country, and lived a roller-coaster life—the opposite of "like father, like son" in our story. But I am forever grateful for the way David and Julie Sewing raised me, along with my two sisters, Carrie and Kris. My parents made their American dream, and at the core of it is family.

For me, nothing is more important than family. It's been a much faster-paced and crazier lifestyle than my old-school parents. But for both me and my parents, our success boils down to our relationships. The American dream is a subjective experience, and so is what we get to say that makes us happy.

My dad found his American dream in the Salad Bowl cafeteria and his wife, Julie Sewing, my mom. I found my American dream with an entrepreneurial journey, building a media company, and engaging my wife, Randee. Next up, family. But whatever the future holds, nothing is guaranteed. The only thing we have is the present, and to be in the moment is the best advice I can give you. Mindfulness has undoubtedly been one of the greatest discoveries of my lifetime. Personal development is an ongoing journey.

Between my old-school parents and me are two very different journeys with very similar end results: we both achieved our American dreams, an ongoing journey, because we never settled, and hard work has always been a worthy ingredient in the recipe.

Meeting new people, honoring friendships, working hard, and building relationships have always been the truest path to success. No matter how much the world changes, that will always be the best way to achieve your American dream. As the world advances in technology, it makes even more sense to double down on human beings, especially the ones most important to you. Don't forget who you are on this journey with, make time for those you love, and be present when you do.

You have a priceless opportunity in front of you. You are alive during an era that will go down as one of the most amazing periods of advancement in human history. The internet is new, automation is coming, and we're still learning how to use both to our best advantage.

The world is changing.

But some things will always remain the same.

If you combine the old-school techniques of work ethic and relationship building with the new-school technology and connectivity, you can create the perfect storm of opportunity in your life. That is how you can "sew it all together."

As I wrote this book, *The American Dream 2.0*, I let it be known to my family that I was sharing the story of the Salad Bowl, a little cafeteria that didn't really even serve salad. But you know what I learned? Elmer Sewing (my grandfather) had the brilliance of mind to give it this name, because just like a good salad, there are a bunch of mixed ingredients.

They were referring to the people and a diverse customer base. And whether it be technology, or people, or a combination of both, in the American Dream 2.0 a little bit of mixture in your approach and relationships, sewing it all together can be the perfect recipe for success.

Find your inspiration, work hard, build friendships,

practice mindfulness daily, stay in tune with technology, never settle, and you will have a chance to achieve your American Dream 2.0.

Thank you for taking some time with me in this book, breathing oxygen into my mission, as well as my American dream. We get one shot at this game of life. Let's "kick fear in the face" and seize what inspires us most. Let's make our mark.

Life is an ongoing adventure, and I look forward to continuing the journey while we walk this planet together.

Cheers to your American dream!

ACKNOWLEDGMENTS

The very essence of a dream is simply an illusion.

One that simply exists in between our own ears.

To make them real, is well beyond what we could ever do on our own.

God gave me life, and aligned me with those I love, and who've inspired me along the way.

Thank you to all who've been a part of this journey.

You know who you are, and with absolute sincerity...

Thank you.

Without you, my dreams would remain just an illusion.

ABOUT THE AUTHOR

CRAIG SEWING was born and raised in St. Louis, Missouri, and believes in Midwestern values. A "college dropout," Craig quickly became a serial entrepreneur working for MTV in New York City, then beginning a successful career in real estate and finance. When the financial crisis of '08 hit, he owned organizations at the epicenter of the recession. Despite adversity, he passionately embarked on a mission to combat negative media. He still fights for the cause today and has helped create a movement, influencing millions nationwide.

Craig is the CEO of Ignite Now Media and host and creator of the company's flagship program, *The American Dream TV*.

CPSIA information can be obtained
at www.ICGtesting.com
Printed in the USA
BVHW072201201219
567383BV00001B/18/P

9 781544 507132